D1409549

# The Oldest Story
# in the World

# Books by Phil Cousineau

*The Hero's Journey: Joseph Campbell on His Life and Work*, 1990

*Deadlines: A Rhapsody on a theme of Famous Last Words*, 1991

*The Soul of the World: A Modern Book of Hours* (with Eric Lawton), 1993

*Riders On the Storm: My Life with Jim Morrison and the Doors*, 1993 (by John Densmore with Phil Cousineau)

*Soul: An Archaeology: Readings from Socrates to Ray Charles*, 1994

*Prayers At 3 A.M.: Poems for the Middle of the Night*, 1995

*UFOs: A Mythic Manual for the Millennium*, 1995

*Design Outlaws: Frontiers of the 21st Century* (with Chris Zelov), 1996

*Soul Moments: Marvelous Stories of Synchronicity*, 1997

*The Art of Pilgrimage: The Seeker's Guide to Making Travel Sacred*, 1998

*Riddle Me This: A World Treasury of Folk and Literary Puzzles*, 1999

*The Soul Aflame: A Modern Book of Hours* (with Eric Lawton), 2000

*The Book of Roads: Travel Stories from Michigan to Marrakesh*, 2000

*Once and Future Myths: The Power of Ancient Stories in Our Time*, 2001

*The Way Things Are: Conversations with Huston Smith*, 2003

*The Olympic Odyssey: Rekindling the Spirit of the Great Games*, 2004

*The Blue Museum: Poems*, 2004

*A Seat at the Table: The Struggle for American Indian Freedom*, 2005

*Angkor Wat: The Marvelous Enigma* (photographs), 2006

*Night Train: New Poems*, 2007

*The Jaguar People: An Amazonian Chronicle* (photographs), 2007

*Stoking the Creative Fires: 9 Ways to Rekindle Imagination*, 2008

*Around the World in Eighty Faces* (photographs), 2008

*Fungoes and Fastballs: Great Moments in Baseball Haiku*, 2008

*The Meaning of Tea* (with Scott Hoyt), 2009

*City 21: The Second Enlightenment* (with Chris Zelov), 2009

*The Oldest Story in the World: A Mosaic of Meditations*, 2010

*Wordcatcher: An Odyssey into the World of Weird and Wonderful Words*, 2010

*The Song of the Open Road* (photographs), 2010

*Beyond Forgiveness: Reflections on Atonement*, 2011

*Shadowcatcher* (photographs), 2011

*The Painted Word: A Wordcatcher's Colorful Guide to Our Mysterious Language* [forthcoming]

*Who Stole the Arms of the Venus de Milo?* [forthcoming]

*How Baseball Saved Civilization* [forthcoming]

# Documentary Film Screenplays

*The Hero's Journey: Joseph Campbell on his Life and Work,* (cowriter), 1987

*The Presence of the Goddess,* 1988

*The FORD V8* (cowriter), 1989

*Eritrea: Portrait of the Eritrean People* (cowriter), 1990

*Forever Activists: Stories from the Abraham Lincoln Brigade* (cowriter), 1991

*Wiping Away the Tears of Seven Generations* (cowriter), 1992

*Ecological Design: Inventing the Future,* 1993

*The Peyote Road,* 1995

*The Red Road to Sobriety* (cowriter), 1996

*Your Humble Serpent: The Legacy of Reuben Snake* (cowriter), 1997

*Wayfinders: A Pacific Odyssey* (cowriter), 1998

*A Seat at the Table: Struggling for American Indian Religious Freedom,* 2002

*The Meaning of Tea* (story consultant), 2008

*City 21: Multiple Perspectives on Urban Futures* (cowriter), 2009

*The New City Ramblers* (cowriter), 2009

# The Oldest Story
# in the World

A Mosaic of Meditations
on the Secret Strength of Stories

Phil Cousineau

Sisyphus Press, San Francisco, 2010

Sisyphus Press
P.O. Box 330098
San Francisco, CA 94133
www.philcousineau.net

Text copyright © Phil Cousineau 2010. All rights reserved.

Frontispiece, *The Storytelling Stone,*
pen and ink drawing, by Phil Cousineau
Copyright © 2010. All rights reserved.

Printed in the United States of America. No part of this book may
be used or reproduced in any manner whatsoever without written
permission except in the case of brief quotations embodied in critical
articles or reviews. For information, please contact Sisyphus Press.

The Oldest Story in the World
Library of Congress Control Number:  2009913967

 I.   Title: The Oldest Story in the World
 II.   ISBN: 978-0-9626548-9-3
 1. Storytelling 2. Essays 3. Native American literature

First Printing: January 2010
Second Printing April 2010
Third Printing June 2010
Fourth Printing August 2010
Fifth Printing October 2011
10 9 8 7 6 5

Grateful acknowledgment is made to the Fetzer Institute for whom
an earlier version of this essay was written as the introduction to
*The Secret Dreaming,* an anthology of folktales edited by Margo
McLoughlin and Ian Simmons.

Book design by WordRunner, Petaluma, California

Front cover design by Gregg Chadwick, *The Poet's Dawn,* oil on linen,
2009 (The Kelly Colbert Collection, Culver City, California)
Artwork copyright © Gregg Chadwick

Back cover author photograph:
Phil Cousineau, Warner Brothers Studio,  Burbank, CA, 2009
Photograph by Jo Beaton ©2009

*This book is dedicated to*
*a great friend and great storyteller,*
*James Botsford*

*The Storytelling Stone,* pen and ink
drawing by Phil Cousineau, 2007

"There's are only two stories:
a man goes on a quest,
a stranger comes to town."

— John Gardner

"I believe that there is one story in the world, and
only one... Humans are caught—in their lives, in
their thoughts, in their hungers and ambitions, in
their avarice and cruelty, and in their kindness and
generosity too—in a net of good and evil. There is
no other story."

— John Steinbeck, *East of Eden*

"There are only two or three human stories,
and they go on repeating themselves as fiercely
as if they had never happened before;
like the larks in this country,
that have been singing the same five notes
over for thousands of years."

— Willa Cather, *O Pioneeers!*

# Contents

# The Oldest Story in the World

# Author's Note

Strange times call for strange books. This short work explores the various ways in which stories have haunted me throughout my life. It is a mosaic of meditations, a rhapsody on a theme, a series of kaleidoscopic vignettes, including myths, legends, tales, verbal snapshots, aphorisms, quotes, anecdotes, pensées, poems and proems, sketches, illustrations, journal entries, riddles and epigrams, and several dashes of humor. Fragments all, but fragments against my ruins, as T. S. Eliot said, splinters of stories from the oldest to the youngest stories in the world, ranging from the steppes of Siberian caves to movies from the popcorn palaces of Hollywood, the Green Cathedrals of baseball to the radiotelescopes of California. Ideally, the reader will experience a progression of voices, images, and ideas culminating in a kind of 360-degree panoramic view of a single subject—the powerful desire to tell and to listen to stories of every imaginable shape and form. The world may not seem to be listening; it may not care. Still, we listen; still, we tell our tales. Still, we write on.

# Part I:

# The Traveler's Well

"Not to know what happened before we were born
is to remain perpetually a child. For what is the
worth of a human life unless it is woven of our
ancestors by the records of history?"

—Cicero (106–43 B.C.E.)

# I

Long, long ago, a traveler was walking across the wild steppes of a far and distant land when he heard the growl of a tiger. Terrified, he looked over his shoulder just in time to see the beast charging him. He turned and fled, his legs straining to escape the fury of the tiger, his eyes searching the horizon for refuge. With the beast so close he could smell its rancid breath, the traveler saw the ruins of an old well with a long green vine growing out of the bricks. The tiger lunged for him—just as he grabbed hold of the vine and threw himself down the well.

The traveler fell slowly, as if in a dream, hoping against hope that he had escaped a terrible fate. But as he fell he saw far below him a fire-snorting dragon, its jaws snapping viciously. Tenaciously, he held on, as the vine shuddered and slammed him against the side of the well. Clinging to the vine, he felt its fierce life force flowing through his hands. Above him the tiger was gnashing its teeth; below him the dragon was licking its chops. His arms were aching, his lungs burning, his thoughts knotting up.

For a held-breath moment the traveler pondered his strange dilemma: everything inside of the well—the shimmering light, the dank smell of the well, the green sheen of the vine—took on a searing clarity. Then he noticed two mice, one black, one white, gnawing at the vine. The sight put him in a rapture. Every molecule of the vine gleamed, as if on fire.

Then the traveler noticed a few drops of luscious honey glistening on the leaves at the root of the vine. Smiling, he stretched out his tongue and licked the honey. Never had he tasted anything so sweet.

Stories matter. Words count. Images endure.

Stories are sparks off the flint of the soul, flares from the cavern of the imagination. Stories are word-fossils, language-animals with long legs. Stories *endragon* the world. They *serpentine* through our souls. Stories are the wolf-tracks of our search for what matters. Stories are wild words on far-flung odysseys. Stories *strangify* experiences and *estrange* the world so we can rise above it like smoke, if even for a moment, to catch a glimpse not only of what is happening—but what it all might *mean*. That's the beauty of it. That's why stories are a means to an end, and the end is meaning, a meaning that emerges slowly with every daring glimpse into your own inward life.

How stories pull off this clever stunt—making sense out of the nonsense, meaning out of non-meaning—is one of life's astonishments. We can explore them; we can even turn them inside out like an old pocket to figure out how they work. But a *deep* story will always have a secret power, a vital force, that we can never fully explain.

The first time I heard "The Traveler's Well" was at O'Connor's, a remote country pub in Doolin, in County Clare, in the West of Ireland, in the winter of 1974. A Russian fiddler, who had hitchhiked all the way from Odessa to play a few reels with the famous local musicians, the Russell Brothers, told the tale around a sweet-smelling turf fire, explaining afterwards that he had read it in Leo Tolstoy's *Confessions*. Twenty-two years later, in 1996, while tramping around St. Petersburg, I spoke with a bookstore owner who informed me that Tolstoy found it in a collection of Sufi stories. Last year, I read yet another version, in a life of the Buddha, while I working on a documentary film about tea, in Taiwan. Who knows where *he* found it? I do know that it reminds me of the old Welsh saying that there are some stories so old that hair is growing on them.

For me, "The Traveler's Well" evokes the melancholy beauty of a saying by the old desert fathers that the reason the desert is beautiful is because it hides a well, which can save your life. The traveler needs to be quick to reach it in time, then needs to slow down to savor the miracle, the sweet honey, of the moment.

Still, like all gripping stories, "The Traveler's Tale" can't be reduced to a single meaning. Its real gift is found in its numinous images—the wild beasts, the dank well, the glistening honey—which are compressed diamonds of meaning in and of themselves. Together, they remind us of a rock-bottom truth. Nothing is as it seems—unless it's otherwise.

If you miss the story, you miss your life.

## THE GREAT ROUND

Twenty-five hundred years ago, Aristotle wrote in the *Poetics* that a story was a complete dramatic action, comprised of crisis, conflict, and resolution. The twelfth-century Sufi poet Mevlana Rumi said that a good story is like the water you heat for your bath. Tai Chi master Sat Hon suggests, "Storytelling is the ancient art of communicating wisdom." The philosopher Hannah Arendt wrote, "Storytelling reveals meaning, without committing the error of defining it." Samuel Goldwyn, the film mogul, remarked, "We want a story that starts out with an earthquake and works its way up to a climax."

This mosaic of descriptions reveals many important components of a story's engine—action, heat, wisdom, meaning, climax—but they miss the one part that helps describe what makes the story leap off the page or screen. The spark that leaps across the gap in the spark plug of a story is *play*, the way a storyteller plays with words, plays with images, plays with time and space, plays with the reader, the listener, the crowd. It's in the spirit of play that we find our voice, our originality, as well as the joy that is the spark of originality in a memorable story. So it's no accident that author Russell Banks uses the word when he pays honor to his chosen profession: "Storytelling is an ancient and honorable act," he says, adding that his "major allegiance" has not been to history as much as to the telling of tales. "[It is] an essential role to play in the community or tribe. It's one that I embrace wholeheartedly and have been fortunate enough to be rewarded for."

What storytellers of all stripes play with is this love of the joy of our desire to solve life's seemingly insoluble problems in a story, to feel it all *click* into place in a great *Aha* by the time we close the book, or the lights flicker back on in the theater, or the bell is rung for "Last call, lads," in the pub.

Not defining, but finding; neither theorizing, nor abstracting, but describing. One reveals, the other transports, and *transport* is the timeless task of the storyteller. We listen for proof of the existence of other worlds, ones possibly more real than ours, ones that make sense out of the nonsense of everyday life. And we soon find our reward is the reverie that comes with the movement of our spirit.

"Tell me the story again," the young Heinrich Schleimann asked the sailor in the Piraeus taverna, after hearing the *Iliad* for the first time. "Well, where's the goddamned story?" demanded Ben Bradlee at the *Washington Post* after Bob Woodward and Carl Bernstein gave him only a rough sketch of what was emerging as the Watergate scandal. "We don't have it; we don't have it," Woodward had to admit. *Not yet*, said the grimly determined Bernstein, without saying a word.

First the story's there, then it isn't, then it's there again. Where does it come from, why is it here, where does it go when we stop telling it?

If you tell it, it's a lecture; if you show it, it's a story.

## THE MOUNTAIN MAN

"Do you have time for a story?"

When we hear that timeless question we have two basic choices. We can glance at our watch and call for a taxi—or pull up our chair, roll our shoulders and prepare to listen intently. We can interpret the offer as an invasion of our time—or as an offer from the gods who just may be offering us a glimpse of the back of beyond.

Asheville, North Carolina, 2002. I was speaking at a creativity conference, and during a break in my presentation sat down in a folding chair so I could autograph a few books. Al Weston, the kindly soundman from Stone Mountain, Georgia, approached me for what I figured was a soundcheck. Instead, he tapped me on the shoulder and said, "You're on fire today, Phil. Do you have time to hear a story about fire?"

I know a knock on the door when I hear it.

Emboldened in a way I'd never seen him before, Al sat down beside me and unfolded an old piece of family lore. During the 1930s, he said, his engineer father worked for the Tennessee Valley Authority, helping to build a hydroelectric dam on the Tennessee River. With unprecedented powers of eminent domain, the TVA made one-time offers to the poor landowners in an effort to persuade them to evacuate before the valley was inundated by the coming floodwaters. One by one, all the mountain folk reluctantly accepted the offers and moved away, except for one old man in one of the remote hollars. After years of cajoling and bargaining with local officials, the old mountain man still refused the efforts to *progress* him, as they used to say in those parts, not if it meant leaving his ancestral home.

Finally, it came down to Al's father, the engineer, to persuade him to move. One shimmering morning, the engineer arrived at the mountain man's dilapidated cabin with the sheriff, two drivers, a tractor with a frontloader, and a flatbed truck. The mountain man was waiting for them on the porch, in a rocking chair, his hunting dog at his side. One more time, the engineer inquired what it would take for him to move.

"Ya'll just don't get it, do ya?" the old codger drawled. "C'mon inside."

Inside the cabin there was nothing more than a hard-scrabble dirt floor, a simple bed, a wooden table, and a fireplace with a smoldering fire, which the engineer thought was peculiar since it was summertime.

"My grandfather lit that fire," the mountain man said. "And my father kept it alive. Now it's my job to keep it going. If I goes out, it goes out."

The engineer rubbed his chin thoughtfully. He was stunned by the fierce truth behind the man's words. There was no sense in arguing with him. There was only one thing to do. He turned to the sheriff and the two drivers, and whispered a few simple directions. They all shook hands with the mountain man, who just smiled, then bent down to light his pipe with one of the cinders in the fireplace.

Shortly after, the tractor driver dug a trench clear around the cabin. Then he used the front loader to lift the entire thing—with the mountain man, hunting dog, and fireplace intact—onto the flatbed truck. With a long blast of black exhaust, the truck wobbled on down the winding mountain road. It did not stop until it had arrived, late in the afternoon, in the next hollar.

By the time Al, the soundman, finished, I was spellbound, the telltale sign that a story has worked. The lights flashed on stage, a signal for us to resume our places. Al nodded, and added one last detail. "My father told me that the old mountain man was a traditional 'keeper of the flame,' and that he kept that fire going until his dying days. Now his eldest son tends the fire. I guess it just refuses to go out."

The art critic John Berger once wrote that any great painting touches upon an *absence* without which we would be unaware of the deeper dimensions of the work, and which would be our loss if we never experienced it. I believe the same goes for great stories. They not only reveal presences, they suggest absences. The flip side of a visible world is an invisible world, which is the province of the arts. For me, it is the difference between the *overstory*, the plot, and the *understory*, the myth, the force, the push of a memorable narrative. The distinction is between what *happens* in a story, and what it *means*, and which is revealed, often unwittingly, when we use visceral expressions like, "That short story by James Salter *deeply moves* me," or that screenplay by Ruth Gordon *deeply touched* me." It's a question of levels, dimensions, movements in the heart.

The story of the mountain man reveals the simplest of plots, but a subterranean current of meaning. We experience a world with fire, and are challenged to imagine a world without it. We discover a man with a strong soul, and are asked to imagine him losing it. The fire is both literal and symbolic; it makes the story endure. Fire is elementally real, but also defiantly emblematic of spirit, soul, immortality, creativity, the vital force. Here, the fire is both the source of heat and light in the hardscrabble cabin, and the connection to the mountain man's father and grandfather, and the land itself.

And as Carl Jung warned, "Never say *just* a symbol."

There is only one story, or two or three, depending on which side of the story you're on. You could be the stranger on the quest, or the stranger who comes to town, or the stranger who greets the stranger who knocks on the sheriff's door. Stranger things have happened.

## THE TRACKS OF OUR STORIES

One night outside Sintra, Portugal, tramping along the cliffs overlooking the Atlantic, I noticed a steep and narrow stone staircase that led down to the beach. My ears were filled with the roar of the sea as I descended slowly between two towering walls of rainpocked limestone, fifty feet high. Suddenly, a gleam of moonlight lit up the walls. For a few seconds, I could see a long track of fossilized dinosaur footprints marching high into the night sky. Then they disappeared, as clouds scudded past the moon, reappeared, and appeared, over and over again, like a cosmic black light show. The eerie beauty of the 100-million-year-old ago tracks took my breath away. I felt inside a taloned footprint and an eon passed with every inch my fingers moved. Vertigo overwhelmed me, as I tried to wrap my mind around the immensity of the upheaval that had lifted the limestone and flipped it over on its side. Reaching for my notebook, I scribbled a few lines, sketched a few footprints. It wasn't enough. I dashed back up the steps and jogged to an old bodega in the nearby village of Penedo. There, I joined a few locals for a glass of port. As startling as the dinosaur tracks were, it just wasn't enough to see it. I had to tell the tale, even if no one was listening, or if no one believed me. No one did. None of them had ever heard of the damned things.

## WORDS OLD AS STONE

When I first read that *bekos*, the old Phrygian word for *bread* was the first word ever uttered by human beings, according to the Greek historian Herodotus, I felt a surge of guilty pleasure because I love words, because I love bread.

When I first read in Bill Bryson's book *The Mother Tongue* about the beginnings of our own language, I felt a wall-to-wall smile crawl across my face: *"This she-wolf is a reward to my kinsman.*" As Bryson observes, this may not be the most profound sentence ever uttered, "but it is the earliest example of Anglo-Saxon writing in Britain," he writes. "It is, in other words, the first sentence in English."

The poet Carl Sandburg must have mulled over the questions of old words and old stories because he condensed and compressed the whole thing, all of classical story structure, down to a three-word poem:

"Born.
Struggled.
Died."

Evidently, Sandburg was proud of himself for this breakthrough because he regularly opened his poetry readings by reciting it to the accompaniment of his banjo.

## THE OLDEST STORY

Often, while lying on a beach looking out to sea, I drift in my mind like Huck Finn on his raft, back to the stories that first fed me. When I was a kid, I loved Homer's wondrous weaving of the *Iliad* and *The Odyssey*, partly because I had read it out loud with my parents and couldn't imagine any stories being older. I've never forgotten reading for the first time Penelope's tender plea to Odysseus, after he had returned to their olive-posted bed in Ithaka after twenty long years: "Come tell me of thine ordeal." Surely, those are five of the most loving, erotic, come-hither words ever written. Surely, that had to be the oldest story on record, the one we tell and retell again, in every generation, in every culture.

Speaking of which, in *The Library at Night* Alberto Manguel tells how the Columbian Ministry of Culture set up a system of itinerant libraries that utilized donkeys with green satchels to deliver books to the most remote corners of the country.

According to one librarian, the books are always safely accounted for. "I know of only one instance in which a book was not returned," she told me. "We had taken, along with the usual practical titles, a Spanish translation of the *Iliad*. When the time came to exchange it, the villagers refused to give it back. We decided to make them a present of it, but we asked them why they wanted to keep that particular title. They explained that Homer's story exactly reflected their own: it told of a war-torn country in which angry gods willfully decide the fate of humans who never know exactly what the fighting is about, or when they will be killed."

But then came the magnificent *Epic of Gilgamesh*, which I discovered in college. The sublimely heartrending tale of the quest for immortality preceded Homer by a thousand years. In April 1840, I learned, a young British adventurer named Henry Layard uncovered thousands of cuneiform tablets in the long-buried ruins of the ancient library of Nineveh, in Mesopotamia. Unfortunately, he couldn't comprehend a single word of it. No one could in those days. Nonetheless, Layard shipped twenty-five thousand clay tablets back to London, where they were buried again, this time in the dark bowels of the British Museum, for another thirty-two years. Finally in 1872, George Smith, a young self-taught linguist and curator, was sorting through the collection one day when he discovered the most famous of Gilgamesh tablets, the tale of the Utnapistim, the Babylonian Noah, and the Great Flood. As he read the ancient Akkadian script he was overcome with joy, shouting to his assistant, "I am the first man to read that after two thousand years of oblivion!" Originally titled "He Who Saw the Deep," the *Epic of Gilgamesh* is the gloriously meandering adventure of the "tall, magnificent and terrible" king of Uruk, the heroic leader who built the mightiest city wall in history, encountered the wise Utnapishtim, and met and lost his only true friend, the wild man Enkidu in a ferocious battle with a terrifying monster. That grievous loss inspired Gilgamesh's quest for the secret plant of immortality. Here is a passage from the end of the first masterpiece in world literature:

> He had seen everything, had experienced all emotions,
> from exaltation to despair, had been granted a vision
> into the great mystery, the secret places, the
> primeval days before the Flood. He had journeyed to the
> edge of the world and made his way back, exhausted but
> whole. He had carved his trials on stone tablets ...

These words could have been written yesterday. That's what's uncanny about great stories. As G. K. Chesterton observed, myths, legends, and fairy tales are more than true, "not because they tell us that dragons exist, but because they tell us that dragons can be beaten." We are seized by stories when we can so deeply identify with them that time stops, space disappears, and we fall like skydivers inside those thin places between the words, and we and the story are one. All my life I've loved that sense of freefall, and the exhilaration of groundrush as the ending of a story gets nearer and nearer, and finally resolves—or doesn't.

There is only one story in the world, and those who hear it think it was written yesterday, and just for them.

## A FAMILY STORY

In the summer of '62, when I was ten years old, my family drove non-stop for twenty-four hours in our new black Ford Falcon, from Detroit to Lake Nipissing, in Northern Ontario, to visit the farm where my father spent his boyhood summers. At dawn of the first morning in our log cabin I awoke to the sound of bluejays in the trees, the smell of flapjacks from the kitchen, and a ruckus out on the enormous glacier rock next to the lake. I bolted out of the cabin to find my father, still vigorous at 34, and my Uncle Emile, ever robust, at 56. My father was staring into a white plastic bucket that was shaking violently. Tentatively, I approached and peered inside just as my uncle was sticking his hand in it. Suddenly, he screamed and yanked his hand out. Red-faced, he held out his hand in front of my face—and now I screamed because it looked like his finger had been chomped off. "The turtle's got it!" he yelled. "The goddamned turtle bit off my goddamned finger!" My father held up the bucket and muttered, "Emile, it's in here." Calmly now, they looked inside, nodding to let me know it was all right for me to look as well.

What we saw was an enormous snapping turtle munching on a long, thin, white, slimy piece of flesh. I felt the blood drain from my face, and began to wobble, and started to turn away—then I heard them howling with laughter. When I turned back my uncle "popped" his finger into place, like the blade of a jackknife slipped back into its slot. It had all been a joke. Embarrassed, I looked again inside the bucket and saw the turtle munching on a long, thin, slimy piece of ... fish.

"All right, Stan, now, let's do it," Uncle Emile said to my dad, as my little brother sidled up next to us. Together, we watched in slack-jawed wonder as our dad stuck his right arm, the one with the bright red "MOM" tattoo on the bicep, into the bucket. Swiftly, he grabbed the snapping turtle by its shell and set it down on a nearby picnic table. Then he grabbed a lead pipe and held it in front of the turtle's mouth.

"Watch this," my father said sternly. "And don't turn away."

The whole world seemed to lurch as the turtle stretched out its long, wrinkled neck—and promptly got it lopped it off like a piece of sausage by my cleaver-wielding uncle. My brother screamed and I yelped, as we stared at the bloody cross-section of veins and gristle. Our dad tilted the headless shell of the turtle upside down and out poured several days of half-digested meals.

"That's life, boys," my dad said, as if he'd just delivered to us the oldest lesson in the world. "You catch a turtle, you make turtle soup."

Then my father did the oddest thing I've ever seen in my life. "Now watch *this*," he said, sounding like Vincent Price in *The Premature Burial*. He grabbed the lead pipe again, and held it a few inches in front of the severed head and neck of the snapping turtle. Quick as a flash of summer lightning, the still bleeding, rigid head opened its mouth and in a kind of death spasm, lunged at the lead pipe and *snapped* down on it. After a few seconds, my father yanked the pipe away then dangled it again in front of the turtle's mouth. Again, the primordial reflexes kicked in, and the head and neck lunged forward and bit down hard once more on the pipe. My father looked victorious, as if he had proved something to himself, or given my brother and I some kind of life-lesson.

If there was a lesson to be learned, it escaped me then. I remember how the incident turned into a story to be repeated time and time again at family gatherings, as if to show how strange and dangerous life was for my father when he was growing up in the wilds of Canada. I remember thinking that I'd never go into the lake again. I pictured thousands of snapping turtles waiting for me in the bottom of the lake, lurching, snapping at my swimming trunks.

In 1996, I returned to Lake Nipissing for a family re-union for the first time in forty years. My mother said something about the snapping turtle incident that helped the story finally fall into place, after so many years. "Everything your father did with you boys had one purpose," she said. "It was as if he was obsessed with turning you boys into hard, tough young men who would never be afraid of life."

## SEARCHING FOR THE REAL

"Their story, yours and mine," said William Carlos Williams, "it's what we all carry with us on this trip we take, and we owe it to each other to respect our stories and learn from them."

Some stories try to make sense out of the distant past, others out of the present moment, still others out of the future. Some entertain us; some distract us; others save our souls. The problem is we usually don't know which is which.

Oh, the sublime foolishness of it all.

On the one side there is the beauty, the luminousity, the great continuity; on the other side, the ugliness, the greed, the great forgetfulness. When I tell my stories or listen to the stories of others, I am making a stand for the first side; when I hoard them my silence puts me on the second side.

Every day I try to find the stories that will bring me back to life.

## LASHING OURSELVES TO A STORY

In *For the Time Being*, Annie Dillard rescues such a story from the archives of the British army's colonial occupation of Papua New Guinea, one that has taken on the power of a modern parable.

> In Highland New Guinea, now Papua New Guinea, a British district officer named James Taylor contacted a mountainous village, above three thousand feet, whose tribe had never seen any trace of the outside world. It was the 1930s. He described the courage of one villager. One day, on the airstrip hacked from the mountains near his village, this man cut vines and lashed himself to the fuselage of Taylor's airplane shortly before it took off. He explained calmly to his loved ones that, no matter what happened to him, he had see where it all came from.

I want to say to that New Guinea villager, "You're a

braver man than I, Gungha Din." I sympathize with him. All my life I've been lashing myself to the fuselage of stories in the hope that one of them will take me back to the distant land that will tell me who I am and what I am part of.

"Yes, this is the plentitude I searched for," wrote Czeslaw Milosz, near the end of his life. "Found not in books of philosophy, or on church benches, or in flagellating myself with discipline." But he says with glittering certitude, "to feel at dawn my oneness with remembered people."

Life happens; stories *mean*.

If you miss the story, you miss your life.

### Reading the Signs

The tilted sign on the door
of the Warner Brothers
animation studio reads:

*Do Not Open the Door:
It Lets the Light In.*

The longest shadow casts
the deepest darkness.

Let it in anyway.

# PART II:

# The Oldest Story in the World

"While the myths of Greece and Rome and the
legends of the Indic gods and Icelandic heroes are
'familiar in men's mouths as household words,' the
oldest stories of all are virtually unknown."

— Theodor H. Gaster, 1952

# ||
---

In late 2008, an old-fashioned blue airmail letter, festooned with an Australian postmark, arrived in my mailbox, in San Francisco. Ally, a friend of mine from Sydney, had written about some curious news that had come her way, and she was certain that it would prove fascinating to me. She wrote that she had read in the local papers that some Australian anthropologists had recently published what they believed to be the "oldest story in the world," an oral tale from the Ngadjonji tribe, the Rainforest People, of Northeast Queensland. The Ngadjonji, Ally informed me, are the "wisdomkeepers" of the oldest culture on earth. For untold generations, the Ngadjonji have been telling a tale about the formation of a volcano on their ancestral land, and recently the crater had been carbon-dated at 12,000 years. If you believe in the long continuity of stories in the Aboriginal world, this makes their creation myth by far the oldest recorded story in the world, thousands of years older than the ones recorded on cuneiform tablets discovered in ancient Egypt and Sumeria. Here is my adaptation of the story she sent to me:

> When the young Ngadjonji boys were initiated by the elders they were warned about violating the taboos. But kids being kids, they ignored the old ways and broke one of the most sacred taboos of all, the rainbow serpent's taboo. Their act angered the serpent's spirit. The old ground of the young men's camp shuddered, the wind howled. The earth twisted and turned. A dark red cloud formed in the menacing sky. No one in the camp had ever seen the sky so angry before. The

earth shook so violently it cracked open. The people tried to run away, but few escaped. The cracks were everywhere, and very deep. One by one people fell into them and disappeared. When the survivors returned they saw a smoking mountain where the land had once been flat and endless.

There is a wonderful old Scots saying: "He who comes to you with a story brings away two from you." Words to live by. Learning about the reputed "oldest story in the world" reminded me of the "oldest road in the world" that I had read about in the *International Herald-Tribune*, in the late 1990s. Archaeologist Mary Leakey had discovered a seventy-foot track of fossilized footprints belonging to what she speculated were a mother, a father and a child who were trying to escape a volcanic eruption some 3.7 million years ago. I wrote up the story and featured it in my short-story collection, *The Book of Roads*, adding a boyhood memory of jumping in my father's footprints on a beach, and my son trying to do the same in mine forty years later. "The Oldest Road in the World" was later anthologized in *The Best Travel Stories of 2006*, by Travelers' Tales, and discovered by the larger-than-life Jeff Dowd, the inspiration for "The Dude," in *The Big Lebowski*. Synchronistically, he had read the story in a rustic hotel in the redwood groves of Big Sur a few hours after taking a barefoot walk with his two daughters in a meadow overlooking the beach. When the girls dashed away to play in the waves, their father watched. "As they frolicked in the surf," Jeff writes in his memoirs, *The Dude Abides,* "Annabelle looked up to see if I was watching her from the bluff above. I was… My eyes got misty as I connected the timeless dots between the mother on the oldest road; Phil and his father; my daughters; my father and me; and oh yes Jack Kerouac "On the Road" to Big Sur. I am gratified that the four girls were also moved when I read them Phil's story as they awoke to another blessed day on our planet." Bursting with excitement over the wonderful string of "cosmic coincidences," the *original* Dude called me several times on the phone before finally reaching me.

"Man," you don't know what it means to me to find that story of yours," said The Dude, "I used to walk in my dad's footsteps, too. And now my daughters are walking in mine, and your son is walking in yours. It's everybody's story, man."

Since I was a callow teenager writing stories and shooting photographs for the *Wayne Dispatch*, my hometown newspaper, storytelling has been my way of redeeming myself, strange as that sounds. I've always been tormented by the fear that I was squandering my time, throwing away the few gifts that came my way. As long as I can remember, I've needed a way of proving myself to some unseen titanic force, my father, my coach, my God. Seeing my name in the byline of a newspaper, or on the spine of a book, somehow seemed to vindicate me, from what I'm still not sure. Original sin? The crime of still trying to impress my long dead father? The shame of missing a few deadlines at the paper?

"Your story's *almost* done? It's still in your *notes*?" my editor, Roger Turner, used to laugh, tugging at his ever-present cigar. "Cousineau, it ain't real till it's ink."

Recently, I had to laugh when I saw how John Updike responded to the question of why he wrote: "To see my name in print." After seeing my name in print more than I ever dreamed was possible, I still wonder if this life of mine is real, or just another story within a story I've made up, or one more ruse to give myself a sharper creative edge. And then comes the ricocheting question, who else lives like this?

But that's another story.

## SHORT STORIES

"Man, he was *hot*," the piano player Bill Evans used to croon after a rousing horn solo by Myles Davis. "Myles, he was telling a *story*!" Hank Williams, Sr. is an unlikely ally for Myles, but he did remark, "A song ain't nothin' in the world but a story just wrote with music to it." And no less than Flannery O'Connor bemoaned the lack of understanding of what she spent her life writing, "I find that most people know what a story is until they sit down to write one."

In 1922, when the archaeologist Howard Carter wedged open the heavy stone door of Tutankhamen's tomb, in the Valley of the Kings, he held his lantern high and stared inside. His fellow explorer Lord Carnarvon peered over his shoulder and asked, if he could see anything. Carter stared inside at the "strange animals, statues, and everywhere the glint of gold," and simply whispered, "Yes ... wonderful things!"

That's me, that's you, that's everyone with a pulse, gazing into the darkness for the strange treasure that might lend some meaning to our lives. There's no telling what we'll find in there, but it's there for the telling, anyway.

In 1959, the Guinness Brewing Company created a rather innovative marketing campaign. They inserted into 150,000 bottles of their best stout a scrolled message that began, "Greetings from King Neptune," and went on to praise the virtues of Guinness to the high heavens. Instructions were included that taught the reader how to turn the bottle into a lamp. Then the bottles were corked, waxed, and duct-taped. Guinness predicted their bottles would be safely sealed for 500 years. Then they dumped 150,000 of them into the Atlantic and the Caribbean. Not long after, 80 bottles washed ashore on Goat's Island, in Canada's Hudson Bay. A group of Inuit hunters tripped over them as they lay scattered on a remote beach in the far north, and used them for target practice. They laughed when they saw the bottles explode, but were mystified by the white-winged pieces of paper that went flying all over the beach. After trying their best to read them, they buried the rest of the bottles in unmarked graves.

Out of respect for the spirits who sent the messages, or fear of the unknown, no one can be sure.

## RIDDLE ME THIS

> Riddle me, riddle me this:
>
> "Black crows on a white bank.
> They are saying, *Caw! Caw!*"
>
> An old Kashmiri riddle for a *book*.

In some mysterious way, every book comments on every other book, every story expands on every other one, until all of human history is one great, sprawling narrative. Citing this old Kashmiri riddle is my way of commenting on the confusion the Inuit hunters must have felt when trying to make out the words they found on the scrolls, and another way of saying the words that comprise any book are no more, no less, than a message in a bottle sent down the river of time.

This is no idle metaphor.

It's the winter of 1984. A seven-year-old boy on a family vacation stands on a pier in Clearwater, Florida, staring out to sea. He winds up like a baseball pitcher and hurls a soda pop bottle that he's sealed with tape into the Gulf of Mexico. There is a simple message inside: "To whoever finds this letter please write me a letter and let me know." It's signed: "Roger Clay, Fairfield, Ohio. December 27, 1984." Nineteen years later, in the summer of 2003, the same bottle washes ashore behind a house owned by a Mr. Smith, in Tampa Bay. Mr. Smith smiles warmly at the boyish innocence, and the charm expressed in the message. Who knows? Maybe he threw a bottle into the ocean when he was a boy. Maybe he's been waiting for decades for a response. So he takes the message seriously enough to track down the Clay family, who are still living in Ohio. He's determined to let Roger know his bottle made it home. But, no, young Roger isn't here, Mr. Clay tells Mr. Smith. "Roger was killed in a motorcycle accident five years ago." Later, he tells a local reporter, "I'm grateful for the message. It was like my son was trying to remind us he was still with us."

These are my *strange pages,* as Nabakov called them, images, dialogue, storylines that seem to crisscross, overlap, intertwine, and link to each other in unpredictable, electrifying, synchronistic ways. What more can we expect from a story? Do we want distraction, entertainment, bewilderment, or something else? My own desire is simple. I hope for transport; I long to be *carried away.* They're intimately connected. The original meaning of transport goes back to the Latin *desporto,* which meant "to carry away," as if across a threshold. It's what we longed for from stories as kids, and what we still secretly yearn for the rest of our lives, to be carried away, to have proof of other worlds, other realms, other realities.

## A STORY TOLD DURING THE AXE-TIME

The Viking sagas tell us that their warriors believed that the finest stories are told around the farmstead fires. While filming a documentary film in Iceland, in 2005, I studied a few local folk tales every day to try and catch the mood of the land. Here's one I've adapted from *Icelandic Folktales and Legends*, which I read one day sitting in a parking lot near the reconstruction of a Viking era farm, outside Reykjavik.

The story goes that during the axe-time in ancient Iceland, the time in between battles, the time of sharpening your weapons,

the time of tending your fields, and hunting for food, four hunters set up camp deep in a valley gouged out by glaciers. Around
midnight, they slipped inside their tent, lying down side-by-side,
in hopes of a good night's rest. The hunter nearest the entrance
woke up in the dead of night and saw a strange blue mist swirl-
ing above the hunter who was sleeping at the far end of the
tent. Suddenly, the blue vapor flew across the tent, as if it had
been hurled like one of Thor's lightning-bolts, and disappeared
outside. Startled, the hunter grabbed his long black walking stick
and followed the blue mist across an open field, stopping where
it stopped, over the skull of a dead horse. Curious, he watched
the blue mist drift inside the skull for a few moments, where it
mingled for a while with a swarm of buzzing black flies. When
the blue mist resumed its journey, the hunter followed across
the field, and down to a babbling brook. Then the strangest
thing happened. The blue mist hesitated for a moment at the
edge of the stream, and stared at the hunter. That's how it felt
to the hunter; as if it were trying to communicate with him.
Finally, he understood what was needed. He laid his hiking stick
across the narrow stream, and the blue mist used it as a bridge
to float across to the other side. The hunter followed as the mist
drifted over the field to a grassy hill, where it hung in the air for
a quicksilver moment before slipping inside. Again, the hunter
waited for the blue mist to reappear, and when it did he followed
as it retraced their journey back across the river, across the field,
and back into the tent. Circling once, twice, three times, the blue
mist settled over the deep-sleeping hunter at the far end of the
tent. Then it vanished with a soft whoosh. The next morning,
the deep-sleeping hunter woke slowly, stretched, and yawned,
and said groggily that he'd just had the most amazing dream.
If only it would come true. The far-rambling hunter who had
followed the blue mist all night asked him what he meant. The
deep-sleeping hunter recounted that in the dream he had hiked
across a field and stopped at a beautiful house filled with revelers,
where he stayed for a long time looking out the windows. Then

he continued his adventure across the field and came to a wide river that was impossible to cross until a gentle giant with an enormous walking stick laid down a bridge for him. Once he was safely on the other side he came to an old burial mound, where the kings of old were entombed with great troves of treasure. He dug around inside, and found a huge hoard of gold. Oh, but how he wished that the treasure he discovered were real and not just a nighttime fancy. Smiling, the far-rambling hunter recounted for him what he'd seen the night before, and said, "Let's go and claim your treasure." Together, they retraced the dream journey to the old burial tomb. Sure enough, they dug up a pot of gold, which they happily shared with the other hunters.

Strange things happen when night creeps up on us. Sometimes it's impossible for ordinary language to convey what happens then, which is why stories, poetry, myths, and folklore proved to be as valuable in ancient times as gold, silver, or iron. In this Viking Age tale, told during the axe-time, the time for forging new weapons, and "keel-time," the time for repairing the long boats, the story unfolds in the mystical voice of treasure stories everywhere. It underscores the secret desire of the waking dream, the revelation that our truest life is when we are in dream awake. This is rendered in the mythic language of the soul, the wispy part of us that wanders in our dreams, the invisible but vital force in us that *sees* into other realms, invisible but vital, and sometimes more real, as the stories would have it, than everyday life. The story challenges us to wake up to that elusive part of us that *sees the dream*, as the Tasaday tribe in the Philippines say. The fiery core within us knows exactly where to find the treasure.

How else, but in a story, can we make sense of where we go when we sleep? How else but in dream-language can we describe what we see there, and what we bring back? How else can I fathom my own terrifying dreams, like this one, scribbled down in the halting rhythms that come from being half-asleep at 4:30 A.M., in April 2009?

> Jo and Jack and I — on an enormous cruise ship — sailing across the balmy seas of Polynesia, bound for Australia — suddenly a storm batters the ship — a tidal wave taller than the ship overturns us — we sink to the bottom of the sea, then slowly rise back to the surface — bobbing like a raft — then sink again, straight down, vertically, the bow bouncing off the sea bed — then rise again — now Jo and I are somehow back in our suites — checking each other to make sure we're all right — then realize our son's not with us anymore — he's still up on the top deck — Jo says she's sure he's all right, maybe he's with some older kids — I nod — we know what to do — we have to climb — I do without looking back for her and lose her around mid-climb, mid-deck — keep climbing, keep climbing to the top deck to find my son — picturing him holding on to the rails, fiercely, determinedly, for his very life — I sense him drenched, alone, terrified, afraid, abandoned, exposed to the storm — I keep climbing, but keep taking the wrong ladders, stairs leading nowhere, false doors — I'm lost, I'm frantic — I can't reach him — I can't save him —

And then I wake up, startled by Jack who's snuck into our bedroom, and is leaning over and whispering into Jo's ear that he's just had a bad dream, where he was "scared of everything, and all alone." I look over at him, in relief, feeling inadequate about my failure to protect him, to save him, even if it was a dream; because I knew he had been in and out of hospitals for the past five months, beyond my reach, beyond my help, beyond my love.

Dreams are stories that know no boundaries, no time, no space; stories are dreams that know how to travel back and forth between the two.

We can think of our dreams as the mere chance firings of the synapses in our brains, or as messages in a bottle sent to us by our unconscious, our soul, the ground of our own being. We can look in them for the thin thread that connects us all, the thread that everything depends on, the thread that is the clew to our survival. We can believe in the awe and wonder of our own lives.

"There is a dream dreaming us," a Bushman of the Kalahari told Laurens van der Post. "I can't tell you any more, but there's a dream dreaming us." Years later, van der Post asked Carl Jung if it was extravagant to worry about how the natural wisdom of the Bushman was endangered. "Oh, this is not an extravagant thought at all," Jung said. "Every human being has a two-million-year-old man within himself, and if he loses contact with that two-million-year-old self, he loses his real roots."

Every night we drift, or part of us does, the blue mist in us; sometimes the other part of us follows, sometimes it doesn't. The difference may be whether we bring back a story, or not. It kills me that my own insomnia prevents me from writing down more dreams that my soul has dredged up from the bottom of the sea.

Consider the marvel of Paul Zweig's insight, in *The Adventurer,* about the irrepressible desire to be transported by stories. There, he describes the uncanny ability of deep stories to lure us into other realms. Those stories deny our nothingness. They help us leap across the abyss between each other.

> Stories may be "invented" or they may imitate the "real" world—one has no trouble recognizing the difference between a fairy tale and a newsreel. But all stories have this in common: they beckon us out of the visible, providing alternative lives, modes of possibility. Merely listening to a story—"losing

oneself" in it—creates a vision of other spaces and times. The story resembles a wind filtering through cracks in a wall: it gives evidence of the vastness. It provides a mobility through time and space, like the magic mobility supplied in old tales by magic carpets and seven-league boots.

Years ago, in the middle of my interview with an old Comanche medicine man on the steps of Chief Quanah Parker's Star House, near Fort Sill, Oklahoma, he said, "*something holy's moving.*" For years, I've been haunted by those words. What did he mean by that startling phrase? Was he evoking the Great Spirit, God, or the gods? Soul or spirit? The force moving in and out of our world we're supposed to remember? What Gerald Manley Hopkins called "the green fuse"? I'm still not sure what he meant, but I'm awfully glad he said it. To this day, I can't read or hear or see any deeply moving story without feeling his words reverberate in my inner ear.

## EVERYTHING YOU NEED TO KNOW

In the early 1990s I made a long journey to Tresbol, a hastily erected village high in the mountains of Northern Mexico, to film an ancient Huichol peyote ceremony with my soul brothers and film partners, Gary Rhine and James Botsford. On the last of our four all-night ritual peyote meetings, I sat in silence around a crackling fire and under the canopy of shimmering stars, along with Gary and James and the Winnebago Road Man, Reuben Snake. Without looking at me, sensing my profound confusion in those years, Reuben said in his signature tough-and-tender tones, "Everything you need to know, Phil, is in that fire. All stories worth knowing are there. All you need to do is watch and listen. A good story is good medicine. It's like our people say, "It takes a thousand voices to tell a single story." And then Reuben stirred the fire with a long branch, and murmured a few far-reaching prayers. He said nothing more until the sun rose over the horizon, when he stood and saluted the fiery orb with a heartswelling "*Aho!*"

Some food you eat and you are still hungry; some stories you chew and you still starve; some gifts you accept and still feel fooled. Some stories matter because they feed our hungry souls; we need to know the difference. There are stories for distraction, stories for entertainment, stories for the exploitation of our loneliness. And there are stories for the approaching thunder, stories told with the sweet living breath of someone speaking across time and space, as if they knew what our hearts needed to hear.

To this point, legendary journalist Studs Terkel explained his motivation for interviewing folks from all walks of life: "People are hungry for stories. It's part of our very being." Novelist and nature writer Barry Lopez concurs, saying, "Sometimes a person needs a story more than food to stay alive." South African writer Laurens van der Post recounted how a Bushman elder once confided to him: "There is the hunger of the body and the hunger of the spirit."

There have been cultures without the wheel, cultures without gold, cultures without trees, cultures without water, cultures without mercy and compassion, cultures without technology. But there have no societies without stories. Who would want to live in one? What would we say to one another? What would we hear?

Once, after teaching an all-day workshop, a student approached me and said that the problem with me was that I tried to find out what was amazing in everything that happened. She said I was crazy. I said I always look for what's strange in a story. She said that was stupid. I said that's where the stories are. She said so what. I said that that's how I make sense out of the world. She said that some things just don't make sense. I said not yet. She said that's what you think. Sure is, I said, I think everybody loves a good story.

Years after he'd emigrated from the Soviet Union to America, the great Russian novelist Alexander Solzhenitsyn sat his sons "astride a rock" on the grounds of his Vermont farm. There, he whispered to them that someday the rock would magically transform into a flying horse and carry them back home to Mother Russia.

## THROW A STICK, HIT TEN STORIES

Years ago, while traveling in Japan, I heard an edifying story from a Zen master, in a monastery in Kyoto. It seems that a long time ago two monks, Tanzan and Ekido, made a pilgrimage to a distant temple. While they walked and chanted the old prayers, a heavy rain began to fall, turning the mountain road to mud. Around the treacherous last bend of the mountain pass, they came upon a beautiful girl dressed in a white kimono that was tied with a red sash. She was stuck, ankle-deep in mud, and couldn't cross the road.

"Let me help you," insisted Tanzan. She bowed demurely. The monk returned her bow, gently picked her up, and carried her across the muddy road.

Ekido was mortified. He refused to speak to Tanzan until they had reached the pilgrim's inn near the temple. "You know monks never speak to women, especially young and lovely ones. They distract us from our meditations; they tempt us with dangerous thoughts. How could you have broken your vows?"

"I felt compassion for her," said Tanzan. "I picked her up and set her down on the other side of the road. Why are you still carrying her?"

As my editor Roger Turner used to drill into me when I was a cub reporter, "There are two sides to every story, and one truth. Tell the story and get out of the way; let the reader figure it out!" I've traced the proverb back to the fifth-century Greek philosopher Protagoras, who said that "There are two sides to every question," and the first mention in America, to John Adams, who used the expression, in an 1817 letter to Thomas Jefferson.

Who knows what ever really happens? We do know some stories sound better than others, some have more fire, some more rhythm; some remind us of things we never knew; some suggest things that never happened but always are. Some are truer than truth. What is sacred to some, is profane to others.

In his book of Hassidic stories, *Souls on Fire*, Nobel Prize winner Elie Wiesel describes a pivotal moment in his youth. One day he told his rabbi that he'd begun writing stories for a living. The wizened elder revealed his genuine disappointment that Wiesel had been telling *lies*. "Things are not that simple, Rebbe," Wiesel told him. "Some events do take place but are not true; others are true—although they never occurred." After some thought, the rabbi replied, "Come and I shall give you my blessing." Centuries of Hasidic storytelling suggest that the rabbi was looking for proof that the young Wiesel had learned for himself that "People become the stories they hear and the stories they tell." In turn, Wiesel, the tireless writer and winner of the Nobel Peace Prize, has come to embody the venerable saying of the Baal Shem Tov, "God made man because he loves stories."

To paraphrase my son's favorite comedian, Bill Cosby, I told you those stories so I could tell you this one . . . .

# Part III:

# The Storytelling Stone

"Stories are predicated upon belief; belief is more
essential to the story than understanding...
the primary object of storytelling is
the establishment of wonder and delight."

— N. Scott Momaday (Kiowa)

# III

———

Long ago, in the time before time, a young Seneca hunter named Crow lived alone in a simple lodge he made from mud and bark. One day Crow was sent out to hunt for food by Old Gray Hair, the elder of his village. Young Crow hunted well for nine days, bringing home a heavier string of birds each time, and offering sacred tobacco to their spirits, as Old Gray Hair had taught him to do. On the tenth day he shot down one meager bird, which he knew wasn't enough to stave off the hunger at home. Frustrated, he stuffed the bird into his buckskin pouch, and set off again in search of more food. He crossed the wide meadow and climbed the high hills, but found no more birds, no game, no food of any kind.

As the sun began to fall, Crow spotted a wide-winged eagle flying overhead. Hungry and desperate, the young hunter followed the eagle to a great river, and there he saw looming before him a dark forest. A chill slithered up his spine. For as long as he could remember Old Gray Hair had warned him about the dangers of what lay beyond the river's edge. No hunter from their tribe had ever ventured into the forest's thorn-throttled paths.

Still, Crow forged ahead. Soon, he found himself alone in a trackless world, for recent rains had washed away every path. But he couldn't bear the shame of coming home empty-handed, and so he walked on until he came across an old woodcutter's path, which led to a small clearing. There he rested against a tall stone.

As Crow sat there, he gripped the bow that had been left to him when his father was killed in battle. Torn between fondness and bitterness, Crow stretched the bow and fletched the arrows, then straightened the points with his teeth. Around him, storm clouds gathered and shadows scuttled across the forest floor. That is when Crow heard an otherworldly voice call to him: "Young man, would you like to hear a story?"

Startled, he looked left, then right, then right behind him. He saw nothing. Feeling foolish, he stayed his tongue, and said nothing.

"Who are you?" demanded Crow. "What do you want?"

No sooner did the words escape his lips than he sensed a strange force coming from the very stone he was leaning against.

"I am Grandfather Stone," said the strange voice, "Would you care to hear a story or not?" The young hunter turned around again, as if trying to get a bead on a spiraling bird in the sky.

A story? The word echoed in his head, making him feel vaguely resentful. He'd never heard of such a thing, and was too proud to admit it. For the first time in his life it occurred to him that there might be things he didn't know.

And so, he asked, "What's a story?"

"Stories are tellings, young Poyeshao," said the voice coming from within the stone. They tell how things come to be. Stories show what happened in the time of the beginnings, the time of the Old Ones."

The young hunter's eyes widened with wonder. He scratched his ear, as if to make sure he was hearing what he was hearing, and not hearing something else. Stranger still, this was the first time anyone had called him by his true name, Poyeshao, which meant *orphan* in the old language.

Leaning forward, the young hunter tried to listen.

"If you don't mind," Old Stone said, "I'll continue."

Crow was still too startled to respond. But it occurred to him that the stone might possess the power that the elders called *orenda*, the force that moves all living things.

"Stories are powerful medicine, words handed down to help us read the tracks left behind by our ancestors," continued Grandfather Stone. "They describe the way things happen, and sometimes why."

Crow grew more impatient.

"Hmm," Crow mumbled. "How do I get one?"

"Not so fast," warned Old Stone. "If you want a story, you need to give me something in return. It's the old way. Why don't you know about these things?"

"We don't have stories where I come from," the boy said. Then he thought deeply for a moment and added, "Give you what?"

"A gift," said Grandfather Stone. "Something in return."

"How about this?" Crow suggested. "It's not much . . ." He reached into his leather pouch and pulled out the skin-and-bones bird he'd shot that day, and placed it on the stone.

"That will do just fine," it replied.

And then Grandfather Stone began to recount the creation of the world. But as spellbinding as the story was, Crow could not stay awake. The words were more of a lullaby than a rousing chorus. Soon, sleep overtook him. With no one listening, Grandfather Stone refused to go on.

The sudden silence woke the boy.

"If you fall asleep, you'll never know how the world began," Old Stone said. "You'll never find out where you came from or why you are really here. Come back tomorrow when you're ready to listen. I will try again to tell you the tale of how the world came to be. I will sing you songs of praise and gratitude; teach you prayers of thanks. Go swiftly now."

Stunned, the boy slunk away, red faced with anger. He brooded all the way home. For the first time in his young life Crow felt a desire to know about the world beyond the wooden lodges of his village. As he ran home, his strides lengthened. Questions gnawed at his heart like a wolf on the bones of a young deer. Why did he have to sacrifice his only bird of the day? Why did he have to leave a gift behind? How could a stone know these things? How would he explain the cold bow, the empty quiver, the utter lack of birds or any other animals? And what about the stone? How could he ever describe what he had encountered in the dark forest?

It was long after dusk when Crow saw the campfires of his village. Slipping quietly inside his small lodge he dropped his empty buckskin pouch on the ground, and fell fitfully into a deep sleep.

Early the next morning, Crow awoke, slung his bow and arrow over his shoulder and set out across the wide meadow and climbed the high hills, searching the skies for birds. When he spotted several partridges flying overhead he let go with a flurry of arrows and brought down two of them, which he stuffed into his pouch, and resumed his journey to the dark woods. When he reached the clearing he strode over to the great stone, and set down the two birds as an offering. Slumping to the ground, he felt happy.

"That will do just fine," said Grandfather Stone.

And then the Old Stone spoke. This time the young hunter was rapt with attention. He listened, and listening heard wondrous things, words that filled heart, words that could not be put into other words. He gave up trying to re-member the exact words of the storytelling stone; instead, he allowed their sounds to echo in him, and take on a life of their own. At dusk, the forest darkened.

When he arrived back in the village he tried to slip un-noticed into his lodge, but Old Gray Hair was waiting for him beside the fire on an old log worn with use.

"Where have you been?" he asked. I've been worried about you."

The boy groped for the right words. "I've been hunting day and night and found nothing. Then I got lost in the dark woods."

Old Gray Hair didn't believe him. Worry raked his heart.

"You were warned about entering the dark forest," he said. "Now you've returned with nothing in your hunter's pouch." I am too old to hunt. I'm afraid our people are going to go hungry. Tomorrow you must find food or we will starve."

The young hunter grimaced, and vowed to help feed the village.

The next day Crow used his splendid bow to shoot down four more plump birds. His heart gladdened as he stuffed them into the pouch that hung from his leather belt. He seemed to outrun the wind as he crossed the meadow and the dark hills and the river, and entered the forest. On the ground in front of the stone he lay down a gift of four birds, along with some sacred tobacco, keeping two birds for the village. Waiting patiently, expecting nothing, his mind became calm as a lake that feels no breeze. Slowly, the sun rose in an arc over the forest. A mist drifted through the trees.

Once again Grandfather Stone spoke, this time with words as smooth as river stones, words as bright as nightblue stars, words as true as moonlight. The Old Stone described how the first winds were tamed, the first lightning ignited, the first eagle shrieked, the first winter arrived, and how the first people were made by the Great Mystery.

The young hunter fell under the spell. He listened, and listening heard wondrous things, words that filled his heart, words that could not be put into other words. He gave up trying to remember the exact words; instead, he allowed their sounds to echo in him, and take on a life of their own.

At dusk, the forest grew strange with shadows. Coyotes howled; wolves prowled. The Old Stone grew silent once more. Promising to return the next day, Crow headed for home, his heart full. Crossing the threshold of his lodge, he dropped his bounty of two birds on the warm dirt floor in front of the fire, and sat down on the log worn with use. Old Gray Hair was waiting for him.

"Two birds? That's all?" he asked.

"Actually, I found more, but—" replied Crow.

"Then what happened?"

"I gave them away, in the dark woods, as a gift."

"Why, when we're so hungry?"

"For some stories, words strung together like birds after a hunt. They talk about things that happened long ago. I'll take you there so you can hear them for yourself."

Old Gray Hair's heart was beating fast. He had no clue what the boy was talking about. He was concerned about the hard facts of hunger in the village. But he'd never heard such strong-veined words coming from someone so young. So he instructed "Legs," his messenger, to inform everyone in the village to prepare for a long trek later that night. They could not waste another day.

Night fell like a sword. The stars wheeled overhead. Everyone was eager to follow Crow into the dark woods. Together, they gathered what little they had in the way of gifts for Grandfather Stone, a few leaves of tobacco, a single pelt, an old string of beads, and two arrow points. As the moon flared high in the sky, Crow led the People across the wide meadow and the high hills, then over river of tumbled stones, and into the dark woods. There they waited so they might hear for themselves the strange stories of the Old Stone. They laid out their gifts. They watched as Crow leaned against the large stone and fell into a trance.

For hours, he rested there, listening calmly, as if to the wind soughing through the trees. To the People, nothing seemed to be happening. They watched, confused, anxious. The stone seemed to be like every other stone they'd ever seen. They never saw it move; never heard it speak. No revelations, no visions, no prophecies came forth from the stone. Old Gray Hair just held up his hand, as if signaling for everyone to be patient, to wait for the young hunter to come out of his trance.

What they could not hear was Crow saying to Grandfather Stone: "We have nothing to equal your gifts, but we have brought you the best of what we do have. We are here only to listen." Likewise, the People had no way of knowing what the stone confided to him: "These are fine gifts, Poyeshao, but you had gifts to give me from the very beginning. You were just afraid."

"At first, I thought I was being tricked," Crow said. "I think I understand now."

"A little doubt is a good thing for the spirit, Poyeshao," said Old Stone. "Too much doubt wounds the heart."

And with that Grandfather Stone began again to speak. Crow listened as if he never heard words before, and in this way he learned by heart the stories of how the world began. When his heart and his memory were full, he opened his eyes, stretched and sat up. Old Gray Hair and his People listened. Crow told stories. He told about the origins of the stars, the clouds, lightning, thunder, and rain, the animals, the fish, the birds and beasts of prey, and themselves, human beings, the clay that speaks.

And so it was that the People accompanied Crow every night for the next four years to hear more stories. The journey became a pilgrimage, the storytelling a ceremony. Those who made the trek learned about the way things are and how they got that way.

One night there were no more stories.

Grandfather Stone told Crow that he had heard enough to last a lifetime. Until the sun ran cold and the rivers ran hot, the stars blinked out and the wind stopped blowing, these stories would save the world over and over again.

"When you grow old," Old Stone continued, "you too will no longer be able to hunt. When that happens, the tales you've heard will guide you in mysterious ways. They are inexhaustible and your people will never tire of them, if the stories are told well and thanks are given. This is the Old Way. Tell your stories as if your hair were on fire. Tell them as if you were entering your village on a white horse. Tell them as if they were the only way you would be remembered by your great-great-great grandchildren.

That was the last lesson that Crow ever had with Grandfather Stone. The boy grew into a man, the man into an elder. He became known as The One Who Tells Stories, The Man with Winged Words, The Young Hunter Who Chewed Off A Good Bit of the Night.

On some nights Crow led the People into the dark woods and sat astride the Great Stone. On other nights villagers and travelers from distant lands and different tribes came to his lodge to hear for themselves the stories he'd learned in the dark woods. Over time everyone learned to bring gifts of fresh game, birds, parched corn, tobacco, beads, bows and arrows.

Those who forgot were asked to return another time.

The People listened and learned. They took the stories home to their own fires. Each story they heard from Crow sounded as if it had been told especially for them. With each story Crow revealed to the People the contours of their own place in creation. With their encouragement Crow never ceased telling the stories. The gifts to him and to his people never stopped coming.

And this, the elders tell us, is how it was and that is how it is and that is how it will be. And this is how stories came to be. And this is how they will last. And this is why we can't live without them.

And this is where our story camps.

# Part IV:

# The Three Hungers

"We are lonesome animals. We spend all of
our life trying to be less lonesome. One of our
ancient methods is to tell a story begging the
listener to say-and-to-feel 'Yes, that is the way
it is, or at least that is the way I feel it.'
You're not as alone as you thought."

— John Steinbeck (1904 – 1948)

# IV

My Comanche friend Vincent Parker once told me that his great-great-grandfather Chief Quanah Parker used to begin his winter storytelling sessions by saying, "Let's move this story around the fire." I'd like to do something similar with "The Storytelling Stone."

First, "The Storytelling Stone" feels timeless. Two threads run through it: the great white silence of the world before stories, and the dark black thread of stories that, once heard, must be retold. What gives it such force? The very word *stone* is a strong place to start. The Seneca have long called themselves "The Stone People," and so it makes mythic sense that Crow learns about stories not from a village elder, but from a rock in the forest. The ancient tongue of myth is speaking here, underscoring a deep identification with the land. The Seneca story rides on the wind of an ancient mystery, the distant memory of the cold stone truth they learned from the very backbone of mother earth. What makes us *human*, it suggests, is being in touch with what is *inhuman*.

Furthermore, what Grandfather Stone offers Crow is something that elders have been offering youngsters since the red dawn of the human adventure. That is, counsel. A rite-of-passage. Life lessons. The sap runs deep in wise elders. It must be tapped. What emerges comes not from intellect, reason, or ratiocination, but from "the spirit world." For this, the Old Stone proposes an exchange, a story for a gift, one kind of food for another, the known for the unknown. Essayist Susan Griffin expands:

There are those who think a story is told only to reveal what is known in this world. But a good story also reveals the unknown. Of its nature, of course, the unknown cannot be fully depicted. It is there perhaps just in the tone of voice, or a style that is loosely knit, and admits thus of other possibilities.

Curiously, in most versions of this story we never learn exactly what the stone shares with the young hunter. Maybe he heard tales about Deer Boy, Turtle's Race with the Bear, Godasiyo, the Woman Chief, How Rabbit Lost His Tail, Kindhearted Lazy Man, Porcupine's Grandson and the Bear, The Forsaken Infant and the Wind, Bald Eagle Sends Mud Turtle Around the World, Genonsgwa and the Stone Coats, or one of the Handsome Lake adventures. And if not stories, then perhaps the Songs of the Corn, Prayers for the Harvest, or Chants in the Night. There are as many possible stories as buffalo on the plain, or salmon in the river. We don't know which stories; we only know that what Crow heard *prepared* him for the life to come.

Therein lies a mystery.

Keith Oatley, a professor of applied cognitive psychology at the University of Toronto says, "If you're training to be a pilot, you spend time in a flight simulator." Similarly, stories may act as "flight simulators" for social life, providing a kind of training, testing, or rehearsal, for real life, for future situations.

The first time I read "The Storytelling Stone" to my then twelve-year-old son Jack he asked me if it was true. He asked in the same voice he'd used when he wondered out loud about whether the heartrending fight between Achilles and Hector in the *Iliad* ever really happened, or my own adventure on the Amazon River, when I ate some grilled piranha for dinner, as I told him, "*before they ate me.*"

"Yes, it's true, Jack," I answered him, "but it may never have happened." Of course, that didn't help much. His face screwed up in confusion, as if he was feeling a little cheated.

"No, Pop, really," he pleaded. "Did it happen or didn't it?"

Justice is a big deal when you're twelve.

Our conversation about the truth of stories reminded me about the student who asked her famous poet-teacher, Andrew Hudgens, "Are you still reading that shit that didn't happen?"

So it was perfectly natural that Jack got upset with my misguided attempt at a subtle explanation. He wanted a true or false, did-it-or-didn't-it-happen kind of answer. Most adults do as well. I tried to explain that life isn't that simple. Myths and folktales, like the best literature and movies, can be truer than facts; they are true in your gut, deep down in the pith and sinew of things. I even told him about Black Elk's famous comment to John Neihardt, "This they tell, and whether it happened so or not, I do not know; *but if you think about it, you can see that it is true.*"

Reading those words I was carried back to the nights when Jack was very young and would turn to me on our blue and white living room couch and whisper, "Papa, tell me a story!"

Are there five more beautiful words than these?

## THE SECRET OF SECRETS

Stories last when they prove to be relevant. The Seneca story reveals a universal, but nameless emptiness that can be thought of as hunger. I count at least three kinds. They stand out, as if in bas-relief to the simple plot. The first hunger is in the belly for *food*, which sends the young hunter out on a search for birds and other game. The second is the hunger of the spirit for *stories,* which is imagined here as the curiosity he feels when he's asked by the stone if he wants to hear one; but it is a hunger that can only be fed far beyond his village. The third is the hunger in the heart for a *gift*, which is hinted at with the ritual leaving of tobacco for the animals he slays, but one that remains undeveloped until the stone reminds him about gratitude.

These hungers are as relevant today as they were when this story was first spun around Seneca campfires countless generations ago. These hungers cannot be measured by science or satisfied in a four-star restaurant. These hungers reflect the longing for another world, the one beyond or beside this one, the one *deep* stories transport us toward. Eventually, all three hungers must be fed—or else.

The secret is so simple it hurts, if you don't know it.

Crow needs to grow up. He needs to become a man. To do that, he needs to know his real story, the one that connects him to the rest of the world, the rest of time. Without your own story, he learns, you never develop your unique life; you are in the dark, living someone else's life. Worse, you are unconnected to the story that holds your world together. To learn these hard truths, the young hunter must venture far from all he knows, as all must do on a spiritual quest. Only in the heart of the dark woods, from a perfect stranger (or a strange perfection) does Crow discover the secrets of the Old Ones, the First People, the Ancestors. Only there in the dreamtime world of a talking stone is he allowed a fugacious glimpse of his "long body," as American Indian elders call the connection to the ancestors.

Stories speak to the orphan in all of us who have been left behind by our family, our village, our world, left, as it were, without a guiding narrative, or what the ancients called a "mother story."

And yet as many of our grandmothers confided to us, there are two sides to every story, and twelve versions of every song.

The old Seneca story is as versatile and tough as, well, let's say it, stone.

On the surface, Grandfather Stone tells the boy that

stories help us learn how to read the tracks left behind by our ancestors; below the surface he is suggesting that the young hunter is hungry because he isn't eating his real food. It suggests that the power of mentors must be rock solid because they are in the business of shaping souls. Furthermore, the Stone of Stories is talking to the "orphan" in the boy, as the boy's tribal name indicates, the desolation he feels for having lived a life in a world without stories. Not knowing our true origins creates the cruelest hunger of all.

"If we don't know where we came from, we'll never know where we're going," Reuben Snake told me in front of the fire that night in Mexico, after our last prayer meeting. "To know the old ways, the old stories, is to know what is most important," he added, "but it requires that we learn all over again how to listen. To hear the old stories is a gift. Unfortunately, people today speak so loudly their own words have deafened them and they can't listen."

"If you want a story," the Storytelling Stone told Crow, "you need to give me something in return." Why demand a gift for a story? Shouldn't a story be free?

## THE GIFT OF GIFTS

"Attention must be paid!" Arthur Miller wrote, famously, in *Death of a Salesman*.

Likewise, in the Seneca story, Grandfather Stone, like all strong-souled elders, insists that it must be *heard*. This is why it goes silent when the boy gets sleepy; he's not listening. Similarly, like grumpy, respect-seeking grandpas everywhere, the stone is annoyed when it's ignored. Moreover, we learn that great, wide-winged, far-flying stories must be earned. Only disposable stories come cheaply. The offer of the freshly slain birds signals that a sacrifice is required for a *real* story, which is one that on some level saves your life. For that, a bountiful gift is required.

Over and over again, the world's great stories reinforce Lewis Hyde's notion, in his ambrosial book, *The Gift*, where he writes, "the gift must keep *moving*." Wherever creativity is regarded as a natural gift there is abundance, Hyde discerns, but if the gift is considered to be nothing more than a commodity, scarcity will reign. When creativity, insight, and talent are hoarded, the community disintegrates.

What is remarkable about Hyde's insight, gleaned from years of studies of indigenous peoples, is that he helps us see that the gift is "an agent of change and has its own spirit." Without the free movement of gifts in a tribe or a community, there is no hope for change. Life is stifled and stagnant. Fear of the unknown sets in, as evidenced by the elders warning about entering the dark woods.

Mythically speaking, our task is to set free our gifts, spread the wealth, and share the treasure because, as the Seneca suggest, a real gift knits the tribe together. When Crow plops a miserable looking bird on the ground in front of Grandfather Stone, it simply says, "That will do just fine."

Implied in the plain language is the plain truth. What is important is the spirit of the offer and the recognition of a transcendent force in the world.

"If power is shown, a gift must be offered," writes Ursula Le Guin, in *Gifts*. "That is important . . . It's important, if you show your power, to offer a gift, too."

Still, there is a knot of meaning here that cries out for some unraveling. To do so, we must plumb the depths of the numinous word *gift* itself. Its roots reach down into the Indo-European word *ghebh*, meaning both "to give" and "to receive," as well as *duty* or obligation, and *provender*, a noble old word for simple food. Thus, a gift consists of giving and receiving, two aspects of the same duty, two sides of the same act of staving off hunger and providing food.

There is a gorgeous symmetry here. To my lights, the etymology reveals a message that is constant to the human race—and constantly forgotten. You are still a child if you only enjoy *receiving* gifts; you grow up when you learned the joy of *giving* them. Thus, the *movement* of the gift is the heart of communal life. The gift that *moves* binds people together because generosity enables people to transcend the impulse to be selfish; it encourages each of us to consider the well-being of the rest of our tribe. This beautiful motif is played out here as a chain of gifts, the bow and arrow for food, the food for a story, the story for the community, which strengthens the strands of the great web of life. All our hungers are connected, even if we can't name them, even if we can't see them.

"Language lends voice to the storytellers who tell us who we are," writes Alberto Manguel. But, he warns, we must remember that there are also stories that lie, stories that don't tell the whole truth, stories that can't keep us from folly, suffering, and mistakes, and greed. However, he adds: "Stories can offer consolation for our suffering and words for our experience. Stories can tell us who we are and what are these hourglasses through which we sift, and suggest ways to imagine a future that, without calling for comfortable happy endings, may offer us a way of remaining alive, together, on this much-abused earth."

## TO LIVE WITHOUT A STORY

What *is* a world before stories? It is a world that believes only in hard facts, only in the visible world, only in the single incontrovertible truth. And it is a world guarded zealously by the official gatekeepers, whether clergy, intellectuals, scientists, artists, politicians, or despots. It is a world that is chronically suspicious of awe and wonder, art and poetry, any expression that defies rational explanation. Our common expressions such as, "That's just a story," "That's only a dream," "That's just your imagination," betray our mistrust of our own inward lives.

Consider again the hungry, sleepy, torpid world of the Seneca that has never even heard of stories, as Crow tells Grandfather Stone. The People long for something more during the long nights; they hunger for more than food, more than the news passed around the lodges. No doubt, there was plenty of everyday information in the young hunter's village, but apparently "no evidence of the vastness," in Zweig's memorable phrase. Something vital is missing in that wilderness of a world without stories.

One clue comes in the telling detail about the young hero's name, which reveals that he is an orphan, in more ways than one, as if he was abandoned by the world he was born into. He was born without a "mother story," an ancient way of referring to creation myths. Without knowledge of how their world began, the tale claims, the young hunter and his fellow villagers have been asleep for a painfully long time. They exist without a vision of where they can possibly go. Such people are condemned to exist under the tyranny of the lone, unconnected, untold moment, doomed to lives of infinite repetition, the terrible fate of never learning anything new under the sun.

Fortunately, as the great Danish storyteller Isak Dinesen wrote, "All sorrows can be borne if they are put into a story."

# Part V:

# In Search of Lost Stories

"Storytelling is fundamental to the human search for meaning . . . The past empowers the present, and the groping footsteps leading to this present mark the pathways to the future."

—Mary Catherine Bateson

# V

In early 1914, a tantalizing advertisement ran in a London newspaper: "Men wanted for a hazardous journey. Small wages, bitter cold, long months of complete darkness, constant danger, safe return doubtful. Honor and recognition in case of success. Ernest Shackleton." Five thousand men applied, dazzled by hopes of glory and fame. Shackleton chose twenty-seven of them. They sailed aboard his ship, *Endurance*, in a bold attempt to fulfill his dream of being the first to cross Antarctica by way of the South Pole. But the furies of nature struck them down. The ship was crushed by colossal packs of ice, marooning the crew for ten months.

With rescue impossible, Shackleton and his men embarked in three lifeboats on a desperate five-day sea journey to reach Elephant Island, which proved to be hopelessly inhospitable. Choosing five stalwart companions, Shackleton set forth in the 22-foot *James Caird* through hurricane winds to South Georgia Island, where he hoped to find help. Seventeen days and 800 miles later they arrived on the island—but the wrong side of it. They had no choice but to march for thirty-six straight hours over treacherous mountains, which had never been crossed on foot, to the Stromness Whaling Station, on other side of island. When the ghostly apparitions of Shackleton and his men knocked on the door, the station manager thought they were local drunks, and asked, "Who the *hell* are you?" The captain of the Endurance said simply, "My name is Shackleton." A Norwegian whaler who had just walked in broke down and wept. Everyone at the station assumed that Shackleton and his men had been lost at sea. Later that night a reception was held in the station's club-house. The captains and officers of the whaling fleets were invited, "old stagers," as Shackleton later wrote, "their faces lined and seamed by the storms of half a century." After the traditional toasts, "all the seamen present then came forward and solemnly shook our hands in turn."

As epic as it sounds, that's not the whole story.

Three years after his return from Antarctica, the nor-mally stoic Shackleton stunned the world when he wrote in his memoirs that he felt he and his crew were not alone.

> When I look back on those days I have no doubt that Providence guided us, not only across those snowfields, but across the storm-white sea that separated Elephant Island from our landing-place on South Georgia. I know that during that long and racking march of thirty-six hours over the unnamed mountains and glaciers of South Georgia it seemed to me often that we were four not three. I said nothing to my companions on the point, but afterwards Worsley said to me, "Boss, I had a curious feel-ing on the march that there was another person with us." Crean confessed to the same idea.

The uncanny silences us, but not for long. Sooner or later we need to recount our life-and-death battles, our passionate confrontations against the rigid indifference of the world. No one is interested in how things stay the same. Few can resist the accounts of those men and women who endure great struggles, and are irrevocably changed by the ordeal.

"Don't tell me the problem," futurist Stewart Brand likes to say, "tell me the story." Tell me what you think it all means; tell me how it changed you or changed the world. Tell me your secret desires and I'll tell you who are. Tell me your dreams, your plans, and your schemes, and how they collided with someone else's, and what you did about it. As Jean Renoir says in *The Rules of the Game*, in one of the most haunting lines in movie history, "The frightening thing is that everybody has their reasons."

But not everybody has their story.

## SO MANY STORIES, SO LITTLE TIME

There are stories, and then there are *stories*. There are traveler's tales, pilgrim's marvels, stories for the stage and stories for the movies, breaking news stories, newspaper stories, celebrity scandals, stories told around the water cooler, discovery stories from the halls of science, bedtime stories, morality tales, love and romance stories, Zen stories and koans, scary stories and suspense stories, and "real life" stories. There are myths, which tell how things came to be; fairy tales, which are stories of initiation or rite of passage; legends that thrillingly combine history and fantasy; folk tales that convey morals with animal character; and parables, stories that are literally "thrown" (*para-ballein*) from the ordinary world to the extraordinary one in an effort to offer a spiritual lesson.

What about the *wrong* story, the one that works for someone else, but not for us? If it's the wrong one, we have to let it go, or change it.

"Don't be satisfied with the myths that went before you," Mevlana Rumi said seven hundred years ago. Psychologist Carol S. Pearson writes, "Those times of depression tell you that it's either time to get out of the story you're in and move into a new story, or that you're in the right story but there's some piece of it you are not living out." "Stories are wondrous," the Cherokee author Thomas King reminds us. "And they are dangerous." If we choose the wrong myth to live by, if we live by the wrong metaphor, if we insist on the exclusive truth of our vision, we may lose our way.

And then there's the prospect of no story at all, the shaggy dog story, the one with no point, no meaning, and funny precisely because it goes nowhere. Everyone's heard someone's site-by-site account of a family vacation, and thought, "But where's the story? What *really* happened?"

And then there's the near-miss story, like the time I arrived at my friend Sandra Hay's spectacular home, high in the hills overlooking Santa Barbara, only to be told, "Hiya, Phil, great to have you here. Oh, by the way, you just missed George Harrison. He was staying in our guest room for the last week while we were working on our film about Ravi Shankar, but he had to leave suddenly—about an hour ago." Over the next few days the words *"While my pen gently weeps"* kept running through my mind.

And here are four candidates for *shortest* story in the world. "Gary's plane went down." Four words; a world disappears. "You're a father." Three words; a new beginning. "Jesus wept," from *The New Testament*; a two-word cosmology. "Lighght," the combustibly controversial one word poem by Aram Saroyan, was awarded a National Endowment for the Arts poetry award, and became one of the most talked-about stories in the annals of modern literature.

"And the candidate for the longest story in the world? Many say the ancient Sanskrit epic, *The Mahabarata*, with its 100,000 verses and nearly 2 million words, but I say the story in this old Canadian Riddle Song stretches even longer:

> I brought my love a cherry that has no stone,
> I brought my love a chicken that has no bone,
> I brought my love a baby and no cry-en,
> I told my love a story that has no end...
>
> A cherry when it's blooming it has no stone;
> A chicken in the egg it has no bone;
> A baby when it's sleeping there's no cryen;
> The story of our love shall have no end.

My old friend, the Irish mystic poet-priest, John O'Donohue, summed it up well for me, as we were walking together in the lunar landscape of the Burren, in the West of Ireland, a few years ago, "You don't *have* a story, he laughed, you *wear* a story. The question is: *Does it fit?*"

## THE ALLEGORY OF THE CAVE

In his classic Allegory of the Cave, Plato described how human beings are like prisoners chained to each other on a bench inside a cave who are unable to turn their heads. Little do they know that behind them roars a fire and between the fire and them is another bench on which puppeteers cavort with puppets, which cast shadows on the wall that they mistake to be a picture of the real world. All the while, just outside the mouth of the cave shines the bright sun, the supreme source of light, which illuminates the one true world.

For centuries, this story has been emblematic of the difference between illusion and reality. Today, Plato's parable is updated daily. The shadow-beguiled character in the cave is now the media-mugged person overwhelmed by the electric shadows cast by 500 television channels, thousands of radio stations, and millions of web pages and blogs. The old audiotape commercial with Ella Fitzgerald begins to sound prophetic: "Is it live or is it Memorex?" The challenge has been amped up and digitalized: "Is it their story or mine?"

Far from being bereft of stories, we are, as the philosopher Sam Keen has said, "saturated with points of view. But the effect of being bombarded with all of these points of view is that we don't have a point of view and *we don't have a story.*"

Far from having evolved beyond stories, we hunger for them, like the villagers in the Seneca myth. But we are living in a time that is overwhelmed with pop culture stories, which *infantalize* us, to borrow movie critic Pauline Kael's great verb. So we should beware, as Nigerian author Ben

Okri, reminds us. Be careful. Tread lightly. Think before you "talk story," as they say in Africa. "Beware of the stories you read or tell," Okri writes, "subtly, at night, beneath the waters of unconsciousness, they are altering your world."

How do we know when we are in a story that is ours and not someone else's? Within ours, the one we most deeply identify with, we are offered an opportunity to find who we really are out of all the possible selves we might be.

The Siberian elders say, "If you don't know the trees you may be lost in the forest. But if you don't know the stories, you may be lost in life." The Cherokee writer Thomas King insists, "Stories are the way that we set the world straight." For Issac Bashevis Singer, "A story to me must have some surprise." Ursula K. LeGuin writes, "I must have a passion to write the story."

Knowledge, direction, surprise, passion. In all places, at all times, in all conditions, people clamor for stories for those four key elements, among many others. From Scheherazade to Spalding Gray, locker room motivators to boardroom moral boosters, gifted storytellers have always held us spellbound as they explained the world to us. We need the facts of science to help us understand *how* the world works, but we long for the stories to discover *why*, and more mysteriously, what it all *means*.

## A POSTMODERN PARABLE

A few years ago, a curious workingman's parable came purring across my fax machine *three times* in a single week. What are the odds? They were sent to me by three of my old house-painting partners, guys with whom I'd painted 44 Victorian houses over the course of seven years of painting and construction work. Here is my own version, which combines the three that came over the transom of my old fax machine:

Once there was an old carpenter who planned to retire. His foreman was reluctant to let him go. "C'mon, let's make one more house together. Then I'll happily let you go and play golf for the rest of your life." Begrudgingly, the carpenter agreed. He put his hours in on the work site, but his heart just wasn't in it. He chose the cheapest materials he could find at the supply stores. He was distracted, drifting off into reveries about his retirement. When the carpenter whacked the last nail into the last wobbly door frame his foreman uncorked a bottle of champagne. The carpenter frowned, ill at ease, just wanting to get away for the final time. Then the foreman handed him the keys to the house, saying, "Here, you've just finished your last house, which is now *your* house. Congratulations. I hope you're happy with my gift to you." The carpenter squirmed, knowing he now had to live in a home he had built half-heartedly.

One version of this urban folklore was sent to me by my one of my oldest friends, a guy from Detroit named Frank, whose copy included a note to me in the margin: "Hey, Couz, sorry I haven't been in touch. I got lost for a while. This story says it all. Hope you get it. Hope you understand. We better make sure all our work is our best work because we're going to live with it or in it the rest of our life. I guess that's the story of my life. Wish I'd learned my lesson in those years we were working together, painting houses till dawn, in the late '70s. Who knows? Maybe it isn't too late."

The Blackfoot writer Jamake Highwater once insisted to me in a little café on Sunset Boulevard, in Los Angeles, that the longest distance between people is culture. But there's hope, he joked, because the shortest distance is a story—which is no distance at all. What I heard him saying that day was that what we are recognizing in a well-told story is our own inward life, our own agonies and ecstasies, our own transcendence and failings. If you do, you may explain me to myself; you may even close the gap between us.

"In this century, its moment and mania," wrote Robert Penn Warren, "tell me a story."

## WHAT IF?

In the spring of 1985 I found myself on the *lanai* of Joseph Campbell and Jean Erdman-Campbell's condo on Waikiki Beach, in Hawaii, swapping stories, comparing myths, drinking neat shots of Glenlivet. Along about midnight Joe revealed that he had been working hard on his book *The Inner Reaches of Outer Space*, and he was determined to include a story he had just heard from the astronaut Russell Schweikert when they appeared together on stage during a conference on modern mythology. For Campbell, the space program was the place to look for the "new myth" everyone was pestering him about, and no aspect of it moved him more than the story of Schweikert, when he was Lunar Module Pilot of Apollo 9, in March 1969. As Campbell later recounted it, Schweikert left the capsule in the first ever self-sustaining spacesuit, with instructions to test several navigation systems and docking maneuvers that were vital to the planned moon landing. However, a technical glitch left Schweikert dangling in outer space for five minutes *with nothing to do*.

"Imagine that," Campbell said to me, his voice rising like a junior high kid, as it always did when he became enthusiastic. "He was hovering out there, alone in space, going *17,000 miles an hour*. Not a sound; no breath of air. Up there was the earth; and out here was the moon." Campbell paused, and went on. "Then Rusty says to himself while floating out there in outer space, *Why me—what did I do to deserve something so beautiful?*"

A wild smile came over the old professor's face. "That's Odysseus hearing the sirens," he exclaimed, "it's Parsifal hearing the call to the Grail Castle; it's the Buddha hearing the call to leave the palace of his father." He paused, and gazed out over the sea. "Imagine that. Five minutes in outer space *with nothing to do!* What would *you* do, Phil?" At that moment, the great scholar of mythology was illuminating the *what if* factor, as all great stories do, allowing us to slip inside the narrative and ask ourselves, in this case, "What if I were hovering in space with nothing to do—what *would* I do?"

Schweikert later said that when he was dangling in the depths of space, gazing back on earth, it appeared to be a "a shining gem against a totally black backdrop." Overcome with emotion in that infinite moment, he said he longed to "hug and kiss that gem like a mother does her firstborn child."

Still, I wonder. Where would *my* mind go if I experienced an infinite moment? That's why the story works. It makes me wonder.

## THESE STONES

Once there was a man who lived for his weekends. Every Saturday and Sunday morning he would disappear from his family, carting his wheelbarrow, and walking with his dog in the nearby woods. There, he gathered the widest, flattest stones and carried them home. These stones he used to lay a path through his backyard, a border for his garden, a sandbox for his children. These stones he talked to, asking them where they wanted to be planted into the warm summer soil. That man spent his week in the office of a tall glass building, pushing a pencil, making myths out of new cars, but he was secretly thinking about his stones, his dog, the woods. He was looking for something out there he could not name.

That stone, that man, my father.

One summer night, lying on our backs on the cool glacier rock on the edge of Lake Nipissing, my father and I gazed up at a Canadian sky that teemed with nightblue stars. One by one he named the constellations for me: Orion, Hercules, Cassiopeia. For each star, he told a story. This hero did this, that one did that; the Arabs discovered this one, the French named that one. He was *storifying* the sky; connecting the disconnected facts of the stars. His voice was desperate to connect with me by way of a story, the only way we knew.

And I was as silent as stone, pushed into myself by the fear of saying the wrong thing and spoiling the moment. And him, wondering all the way to the grave if I ever listened to him.

Twenty years later, in the spring of 1985, with only weeks to live, he wrote to me with a red marker on a simple index card that he had slipped inside an old LIFE magazine: *"Did my love of words influence you?"*

He died before I could answer him.

Who knows the effect our words have on others? Did Shackleton know his preternaturally calm words would outlive him, the ones that had staved off mutiny, soothed his crew, and got every last man home? Did Schweikert know that his single drifting sentence—*Five minutes with nothing to do*—would come to symbolize a sacred dimension of the space program?

## IT'S ALL ONE STORY

In October 2009, I visited the Baseball Hall of Fame, in Cooperstown, New York to do some research for an upcoming book. I met with Jim Gates, the head librarian, who gave me the VIP tour, including a meander through the underground vault where he allowed me to swing Babe Ruth's famous notched bat. While down there, Jim regaled me with one of the most of the unusual baseball stories I've ever heard. During World War II, he told me, an American G.I. from Grand Rapids, Michigan, named Tommy Thomas, was captured by the Japanese in the Philippines and incarcerated in the Cabanatuan prison camp after the Bataan Death March, for what he called three excruciatingly tedious years. To break the monotony, the American prisoners practiced myriad forms of daydreaming, from conjuring up elaborate meals to debating whether or not a possum has two penises. For Thomas, one of the most enjoyable distractions, when he didn't have work duty, was to sneak over to the Section 8 medical ward. There, he often joined his fellow prisoners under the window of an eccentric baseball-obsessed fan who gave impromptu baseball "broadcasts." His games always featured the Cubs versus the Giants, for reasons no one ever figured out, and the play-by-play was so realistic the camp prisoners leaned on his every word, as if listening to their favorite radio announcers back home. Those who arrived after the first pitch would ask, "What inning is it?"

Fascinating, but for me not the whole story. Thomas was in the camp to help the prisoners escape. Twenty-seven years later, in 1981, I was searching for my missing brother in villages along the road from Clark Air Force Base, outside Manila, and stopped by the site of the old prison camp. Months later, I found him far away, safe and sound, in the *bundoks*, the mountains of northern Luzon, protected by local Filipinos. They helped him in the same spirit in which they helped the escapees from the Japanese prison camps. "When a man enters my village," one of his protectors told me, "he is my brother."

A coda: *bundok* was remembered as *boondocks* by the same G.I.s who escaped the camps, a word used to describe the farthest outposts of civilization, and later a famous homerun call by Tigers announcer Ernie Harwell. "Horton hits one deep, deep—way out in the boondocks!" Where did he hear it? As the 2009 baseball season was winding down, we spoke by telephone and Ernie told me that when he was in the Marines his drill instructor used the word to describe where he hid out during the last months of World War II, in the *bundoks* of the Philippines.

Stories have a life of their own; like subatomic particles they seem to come and go as they please. As the man in the haunted ink bottle said, it's all one story. Or as Jim Gates told me, "As we say around here, it all comes back to baseball."

## THIS MUCH I KNOW

Every day we have at least one gut-check moment. Every day we are asked, *"Do you want to hear a story?"* A hundred times a day our deeper life awaits our signal that, yes, we are listening. Whether we are camped around a fire on the Comanche Moon trail, sitting in the literary salons of Gertrude Stein and Alice B. Toklas on the Rue des Fleurs in Paris, craning our necks during a Hollywood studio script meeting, cosseting our children by reading out loud to them from the great round of Harry Potter adventures, or trading old baseball stories in the stands with old teammates, we are responding to the blue longing in our restless souls to be *carried away* by the kind of story that makes life worth living.

"That's the way things come clear," wrote Madelaine L'Engle, winner of the Newbery Medal for children's literature. "All of a sudden. And then you realize how obvious they've been all alone."

"Two things make a story," said Chilean poet Pablo Neruda. "The net and the air that falls through the net."

"The world is made up of stories, not atoms," remarked the American poet Muriel Rukeyser.

"The story is his adventure in search of a hidden truth," wrote Raymond Chandler of his character, Philip Marlowe, "and it would be no adventure if it did not happen to a man fit for adventure."

When asked why he wrote stories, Vladimir Nabakov said, "I don't wish to touch hearts. I don't even want to effect minds very much. What I really want to produce is that little sob in the spine of the artist-reader."

"A word has power in and of itself," writes the Kiowa story-teller and scholar N. Scott Momaday. "It comes from nothing into sound and meaning; it gives origin to all things. By means of words can a man deal with the world on equal terms. And the word is sacred."

Word by word, image by image, memory by memory, we accumulate stories on our journey through life that tell us who we are and how we fit into the greater story. The journey that began with our ancestors long ago at the edge of the old world as carried on, like churning white water down the course of a river, now carries us. And we keep them moving in our own writing, catching up over holiday meals with stories of loved ones, swapping stories and brag-book photos of our kids at children's playgrounds, by finding the robust narrative that gives movement to our ideas in politics, or, sadly, in eulogies at the funerals of our close friends.

This is how we carry on. By pushing our raft of stories down the river of life so we can understand ourselves, and each other better than if we lived in stone-cold silence. When folks ask what I mean when I say stories save our souls, that is what I tell them; stories save us when they heal us from the pain of living without a raft, without meaning, without knowing where we're going.

To paraphrase Goethe, when the mind is at sea, a new story provides a raft.

Life happens; stories *mean*.

## THE STORY OF THE UNIVERSE

My friend, cosmologist Brian Swimme, has thought long and hard about the changing role of the story in the wake of the miraculous discoveries of modern science.

"What will happen when the storytellers emerge?" he asks. "They will sing our epic of being, and stirring up from our roots will be a vast awe, an enduring gratitude, the astonishment of communion experiences, and the realization of the cosmic adventure."

To explore this emergence, in the early 1990s, Swimme co-founded a think tank in the Bay Area called "The Story of the Universe" that I participated in for a few years. One of our most memorable meetings was with Jane Goodall, who came to speak about her work with chimpanzees at Gombe National Park, in Tanzania. Her plea for the preservation of the chimpanzee's way of life was brilliant, but what moved me most was hearing her speak about the first time she encountered their "waterfall displays." She had been hiking in the Gombe forest, and came across a waterfall that tumbled 80 feet on to the rocks below. There, she told us, she encountered a group of chimpanzees performing rhythmic dances, backflips, leaps from foot to foot, and even throwing rocks at the waterfall. She crawled close enough to the chimps to see the hair standing on their arms when they stared at the waterfall.

Years later, in 2003, I heard her delve deeper into the story, at the Commonwealth Club, in San Francisco. "If they had this spoken language," she said, "if they could sit down and talk about the feelings of what must be something akin to awe and wonder that triggers these amazing displays, then that might turn to one of the early human religions, the animistic religion, worship of water and sun and moon and elements that they couldn't understand. But that leads me on to my belief that there is a great spiritual power out there, and it's a spiritual power from which I believe that I can draw strength."

The oldest story is the first one that evoked awe and wonder.

## WHAT NOW?

In the spring of 2009 I was one of the lecturers aboard the Silver Shadow, a handsome ship that sailed across Polynesia, from Hawaii to New Zealand. My fellow lecturer was the raffish Irish writer and raconteur, Frank McCourt. The night before we docked at Christmas Island, Frank and his wife Ellen invited me to join them on deck for a Polynesian barbecue dinner. While sipping our iced teas we talked about the writing life. He told me that he had grown up in Ireland among wonderful storytellers, but when he came to America what he wanted to do more than anything was to teach high school English, so he could help kids tell their stories. For thirty-six years, he did just that, becoming a legendary teacher in the New York public school system. On his last day of classes his students presented him with a pen, saying, "Now it's your turn, teacher man."

McCourt was lucky. Not everybody gets his turn. Over the next twelve years, he wrote *Angela's Ashes*, *Tis'*, and *Teacher Man*. That night on the ship he also told me he had been writing for a few hours every night on the ship, trying to finish his fourth novel, which he described unsentimentally as "the toughest work of my life." The next day, after exploring the island, he had a seizure while boarding the ship that he never fully recovered from.

Since Frank's passing I've been haunted by that line about it being "your turn, teacher man," which was his student's affectionate nickname for him. The words have been reverberating in me like an Irish reel you can't get out of your head. I keep thinking about what it means to have your turn in life. Every day we have stories pressing in on our heart that are dying to get out, desperate to be told. Of all the stories we can tell or read or listen to, which ones will we choose? If there is only one story, as John Gardner insisted, it shouldn't be that hard to decide. But if it's two or three, as Flannery O'Connor said, that complicates things. If it's more, like the innumerable stories McCourt was racing against the clock to get down on paper, well, what do we do then?

We try to get them down, one at a time, as they came to us.

*When it's ink, it's real.*

Do you have time for one more story? I have a friend in County Clare, Ireland who believes that stories are the music of our lives. P. J. Curtis is a musicologist, record producer, author, poet, and ex-Airforce man stationed in Borneo during the harrowing Borneo-Indonesia war of 1964-65. Recently, he sent me a marvel of a story that I thought I'd actually lived through, in some *wyrd* way, in the original sense of *wyrd* referring to strange twists of *fate*. In 1963, he returned home from Borneo by a curious concatenation of vehicles, including ship, plane, train, and for the final stretch, in the donkey cart of a local farmer, Tom Neylon. When he arrived home he was hoping his father would be impressed by his exotic itinerary, but his father remained unmoved, and worse, unimpressed until P. J. told him about being rescued by the farmer, the ass, and the cart.

"Did Tom give you any old story *atal*?" his father asked. "That man has a story for every day of the year!" At that moment Curtis realized that what mattered to his father was that his son came home armed with a good story, preferably one that he had not heard, and especially one from the local gifted storyteller who carried hundreds of mesmerizing stories in his head.

"Tom had indeed a story for every day of the year," writes Curtis, "and he had indeed regaled me with several stories as we clopped along the starlit road. I didn't know it then, but now— all these decades on— I realize that my father's response taught me a valuable lesson on what lies at the heart of every journey. However fantastic, however humble or however mundane it may be, a journey without a story told is a journey incomplete. Only when a story is gathered on the road and re-told on arrival can it be said that the traveler has truly made a journey home."

Uncanny, I thought when I read Curtis' letter, just uncanny.

In 1980, I lived in Ballyconneelly, Connemara, Ireland, not far from where he lives, in County Clare. I spent a few evenings with a local bachelor named Tommy, who was nearly a hundred-years-old. Old Tommy, as we called him, had lived in the same thatched-roof, whitewashed cottage all his life. Since he rarely went "down pub," his one form of entertainment was "telling the tall ones," the old Irish myths, to the local children, and to the chance traveler who came knocking on his door. One day I asked Tommy of all the stories he knew which one was his favorite story? "The Wooing of Befola," "The Enchanted Cave of Cesh Corran," or "The Twelve Wild Geese"?

"Aye, lad, I do have a favorite story," he said in a bog-deep brogue, "and my favorite is the one and only story, the oldest story in the world, a story so old you know it before you hear it. The oldest story is the one about the traveler who meets himself coming home and doesn't recognize himself, until he sits down with himself and hears himself tell himself what happened while he was away. Himself is the traveler who returns home to tell about it. Aye, that's my favorite. Now, will ye have a cuppa tea with me, lad?"

It was long ago that this would happen again, here in the story I am writing and you are now reading.

And if that doesn't work for you, if you don't like the stories you're hearing, reading, or seeing, all the ones that came before you, and are swarming around you now, go deeper; go out and live one of your own. Then tell me about it.

*Phil Cousineau*
*San Francisco – Olympia, Greece*
*September 2005 – September 2009*

# Epilogue

"The story has been told.
If it was beautiful then it belongs to everyone;
if it was bad it belongs to me only;
That is my fault, the storyteller."

— Zanzibar Swahili saying

Long ago, a prestigious conference of religious scholars was held in a faraway land. The meeting began with a vigorous and combustible theological debate, the kind that never fails to separate thinkers and believers. The longer they argued the deeper the wedges were driven into their already fractious faith. After all, you can't teach an old dogma new tricks. Finally, a break was called. The call went out for the speakers' papers to be handed in, assembled, collated, and stacked on tables in the hallways, where they went largely unread.

On the last morning of the conference, a sunny Sunday, a brief seminar was offered to the actual practitioners of all faiths represented at the conference. For this gathering there was no debate; there wasn't even any talking. What evolved was the long-rumored, highly elusive, silent dialogue. As quiet as church mice, the practitioners sat around a large round table smiling at each other. They nodded their heads. They laughed until they cried. They laughed in a hundred accents. They laughed in common.

Words, words, words.

And all the silence in between.

Silence, too, is a story.

In a word.

# Recommended Reading

Bryson, Bill. *The Mother Tongue*. New York: Harper Perennial, 1991.

Curtis, P. J. *The Lightning Tree*. Kerry, Ireland: Brandon Press, 2006.

DeLoria, Jr. Vine. *For This Land: Writings on Religion in America*. London and New York: Routledge, 1998.

Dillard, Annie. *For the Time Being*. New York: Vintage Books, 2000.

Fry, Rodney. Ed. *Stories That Make the World: Oral Literature of the Indian Peoples of the Inland Northwest. As Told by Lawrence Aripa, Tom Yellowtail, and Other Elders*. Norman, OK: University of Oklahoma Press, 1995.

Gaster, Theodor H. *The Oldest Stories in the World*. Boston: Beacon Books, 1952.

Granta magazine 21: *The Storyteller*. London: England, 1987.

Griffin, Susan. *A Chorus of Stones: The Private Life of War*. New York: Doubleday Publishing, Inc., 1992.

Hawthorne, Nathaniel. *Twice-Told Tales*. New York: The Heritage Press, 1936.

Highwater, Jamake. *The Primal Mind: Vision and Reality in Indian America*. Harper Collins, 1983.

Hyde, Lewis. *The Gift: Imagination and the Erotic Life of Property*. New York: Vintage Press, 1983.

Keen, Sam, with Anne Valley-Fox. *Your Mythic Journey: Finding Meaning in Your Life Through Writing and Storytelling*. Santa Barbara, CA.: Jeremy P. Tarcher, Publishers, 1989.

King, Thomas, *The Truth About Stories*. Minneapolis, MN.: The University of Minnesota Press, 2005.

Le Guin, Ursula. *Gifts*. New York: Harcourt, Inc., 2004.

Manguel, Alberto. *The City of Words*. Toronto, Ont.: The House of Anansi Press, Inc., 2007.

————————. New Haven, CT.: *The Library at Night*. Yale University Press, 2008.

McKee, Robert. *Story: Substance, Style, and The Principles of Screenwriting*. New York: Harper Collins, 1997.

Momaday, N. Scott, *The Way to Rainy Mountain*. Albuquerque, NM: University of New Mexico Press, 1969.

Simpson, Jacqueline (translator and editor). *Icelandic Folk Tales and Legends*. Berkeley: University of California Press, 1979.

Weisel, Elie. *Souls on Fire: Portraits and Legends of Hasidic Masters*. New York: Simon and Schuster, 1982.

Zweig, Paul. *The Adventurer*, Princeton, NJ: Princeton University Press, 1974.

# Acknowledgments

*"A gift goes out on a donkey
and comes back on a camel."*
— Egyptian proverb

First and foremost, I wish to acknowledge Mark Nepo and Angeles Arrien of the Fetzer Institute, in Kalamazoo, Michigan, for commissioning me to write the introduction for *The Secret Dreaming*, an anthology of folk tales about the role of the gift in human history. The collection reflects an abiding faith in the intricate web of connections between stories, gifts and community and it influenced and inspired me to expand that brief introduction into this essay. I would also like to express my gratitude to several other strong influences, including the late Reuben Snake (Ho-Chunk-Winnebago), Walter Echo-Hawk (Pawnee), Vine Deloria, Jr. (Dakota Sioux), Tanya Frichner (Onondaga), Joanne Shenandoah (Onondaga), Douglas George-Kanentiio (Mohawk-Iroquios), Hayna Brown (Winnebago), Vincent Parker (Comanche). I also want to express my ongoing thanks to Brian Swimme, Bruce Bochte, Joe Meeker, and Stuart Brown at "The Story of the Universe." It was a privilege and a joy to explore the cosmic dimensions of story with you. One other influence should not pass unmentioned, my father, Stanley H. Cousineau, whose library, which I inherited, continues to stoke my storytelling fire. To inspire this expanded work I read and reread his copies of *Kim, Moon for Sixpence, Twice-Told Tales, The Tall Tales of Paul Bunyan*, and others, and was doubly convinced about the worth of an essay on the power of deep story. And special thanks as well to a man I am proud to call a friend, the Hall of

Fame baseball broadcaster, Ernie Harwell, whose voice and stories, humility and grace, have been a life-long inspiration.

I would also like to raise a cup of strong espresso to the baristas at Caffé 901 Columbus, in North Beach, where the stories in this book were burnished. And I want to express my abiding gratitude to my wife Jo, who read umpteen versions of this manuscript and offered beaucoup advice and honest encouragement, and to my son Jack Cousineau, now thirteen. In the summer of 2008, when we were on our own odyssey around the Greek islands Jack provided me with the golden thread that got me through this labyrinthine essay: "A story is the presentation of a memorable experience that makes you feel like you've traveled to another world—or you long to do so." His description would make our voyageur ancestors proud.

Finally, I need to acknowledge two soul brothers, Gregg Chadwick, whose stunning painting, *The Poet's Dawn*, graces the cover of *The Oldest Story in the World*, and James Botsford (North Dakotan-Wisconsin) for years of friendship, joke-spinning, beer-sampling, and story-swapping.

Rhino would be proud.

# About the Author

Phil Cousineau is a freelance writer, independent filmmaker, photographer, worldwide lecturer, travel leader, and storyteller. For the last thirty years he has published a Huck's raft worth of books on such topics as creativity, soul, movies, sports, and the mythic imagination. Cousineau was born in an army hospital in South Carolina, and raised in Detroit, the same stubbornly independent soil that gave rise to the soulful work of Bob Seger, Smoky Robinson, Phillip Levine, Elmore Leonard, Lily Tomlin, Jim Harrison, and Al Kaline. Among Cousineau's many books are *Stoking the Creative Fires*, and The *Olympic Odyssey: Rekindling the Spirit of the Ancient Games*, which was selected by the United States Olympic Committee and given to all 1700 American athletes at the 2004 Summer Games in Athens, The *Art of Pilgrimage*, and *Night Train*, which was illustrated by his son Jack. His documentary film credits include the modern classic, *The Hero's Journey: The Life and Work of Joseph Campbell*, *The Peyote Road;* and *Forever Activists: Stories from the Abraham Lincoln Brigade* (1991 Academy Award nominated). Currently, Cousineau is a Fellow of the Joseph Campbell Foundation, and host of LINK TV's national television series, "Global Spirit." He lives with his family on the much bestoried Telegraph Hill, in San Francisco, where he coaches youth baseball on the same sandlot where the DiMaggio brothers grew up playing ball, and trading stories like baseball cards.

# Colophon

*The Storytelling Stone* was designed and typeset by Jo-Anne Rosen of Wordrunner Publishing Sevices in Petaluma, California. The text typeface Chaparral Pro, created by Adobe type designer Carol Twombly, combines the legibility of slab serif designs popularized in the 19th century with the grace of 16th-century Roman book lettering. Chaparral has varying letter proportions that give it an accessible and friendly appearance in all weights from light to bold. The titles and headers are set in ITC Stone Sans, designed by Sumner Stone in 1987. ITC Stone Sans is a modern version of the "humanistic" sans-serif subcategory. *The Oldest Story in the World* was printed and bound by Gorham Printing in Centralia, Washington in an edition of 250 copies. Front cover design is by Gregg Chadwick.

# To Order More Books

For more copies of *The Oldest Story in the World* or other books and documentary films by Phil Cousineau, please write to:

Sisyphus Press
P.O. Box 330098
San Francisco, CA 94133

Or email: pilgrimage@earthlink.net

Information about Phil Cousineau's other books, films, lectures, and literary tours may be found at:
www.philcousineau.net